BEGINNING

DRUMSET

The Complete Drumset Method

Beginning • Intermediate • Mastering

PETE SWEENEY

Alfred, the leader in educational publishing, and the National Guitar Workshop, one of America's finest guitar schools, have joined forces to bring you the best, most progressive educational tools possible. We hope you will enjoy this book and encourage you to look for other fine products from Alfred and the National Guitar Workshop.

Alfred Publishing Co., Inc.
16320 Roscoe Blvd., Suite 100
P.O. Box 10003
Van Nuys, CA 91410-0003
alfred.com

ISBN-10: 0-7390-3474-X (Book & CD)
ISBN-13: 978-0-7390-3474-3 (Book & CD)

This book was acquired, edited and produced
by Workshop Arts, Inc., the publishing arm of the National Guitar Workshop.
Nathaniel Gunod: acquisitions, managing editor
Ante Gelo: music typesetter
Timothy Phelps: interior design
CD recorded at Bar None Studios, Northford, CT
Cover photograph: Karen Miller

TABLE OF CONTENTS

ABOUT THE AUTHOR 3

INTRODUCTION 4

THE DRUMSET 5

CHAPTER 1—BASIC TERMINOLOGY AND NOTE VALUES 6

The Staff, Measures and Time Signatures 6
Note Values 7
Note and Rest Value Tables 8
The Metronome and Reading Exercises 9
Drumset Notation 11

CHAPTER 2—SNARE DRUM TECHNIQUE 12

Holding the Sticks 12
Basic Stroke Technique 13
Rudiment: Single-Stroke Roll 14
Rudiment: Double-Stroke Roll 15
Rudiment: The Paradiddle 16
Short-Roll Combinations 17
Snare Drum Solo 19

CHAPTER 3—ACCENT STUDIES AND DYNAMICS 20

Four Basic Movements 20
Combination Studies 22
Dynamics 27

CHAPTER 4—BASIC DRUMSET COORDINATION: ROCK BEATS 29

The Bass Drum 29
The Hi-Hat 30
Snare, Bass Drum and Hi-Hat Rock Beats 32
Changing the Hi-Hat Sound 37
Syncopated Beats 41
Half-Time Rock Beats 42
Double-Time Rock Beats 43
Stepping the Hi-Hat; The Ride Cymbal 44

CHAPTER 5—MORE EIGHTH-NOTE ROCK 46

Practice Considerations for the 20 Beat Patterns and Bass-Drum Reading Source 50

CHAPTER 6—INTRODUCING SIXTEENTH NOTES 51

Sixteenth-Note Transition Exercises 52
Sixteenth-Note Reading Exercises 53
Sixteenth-Note Accent Studies 56
Applying Accents to the Drumset 58

CHAPTER 7—GETTING AROUND THE DRUMSET 59

Bass Drum and Snare Drum Workout 59
Moving Around the Set with Single Strokes 61
Moving Around the Set with Double Strokes 63
Hand and Foot Combinations Around the Set 64
The Crash Cymbals and Single-Strokes 65

CHAPTER 8—SIXTEENTH-NOTE BEATS 68

Sixteenth-Note Hi-Hat Beats 69
Adding Sixteenth Notes to the Snare Drum 71
Adding Sixteenth Notes to the Bass Drum 72
Eighth-Note Hi-Hat with Mixed Sixteenth-Note Beats 73
Changing Sixteenth-Note Rhythms Into Beats 74
Dotted Notes 76
Two Sixteenth Notes on the Bass Drum 78
Playing Offbeats on the Bass Drum 80
Single Sixteenth-Note Bass-Drum Exercises 82
Double Sixteenth-Note Bass-Drum Exercises 83
Progressive Sixteenth-Note Bass-Drum Exercises 84

CHAPTER 9—GETTING STARTED WITH DRUM FILLS 85

Developing the Four-bar Phrase 86
The Eighth-Note Flow for Drum Fills 87
Eighth-Note Fills that End on Beat 4 88
Short Fills Using Sixteenth Notes 89
Longer Fills Using Sixteenth Notes 91
Resolving Fills on the "&" of Beat 4 93

APPENDIX—JOE MORELLO INTERVIEW: PART 1 94

ABOUT THE AUTHOR

Pete Sweeney has been a professional musician since 1983. He studied with Dave Calarco and Joe Morello and attended the Drummer's Collective in New York City.

Pete has been a faculty member at the National Guitar Workshop since 1993. He has performed with many great musicians such as "Dangerous" Dan Toler, Duke Robillard, Mick Goodrick, Larry Coryell, Nick Brignola, Cary DeNigris and Frank Gambale. He has performed concerts with Robben Ford, Andy Summers (formerly of the Police), and Laurel Masse (of the Manhattan Transfer). Pete has performed on two Grammy nominated CDs with Jay Traynor and the Joey Thomas Big Band, and can be heard on the soundtrack of the Mirimax film "The Castle."

Pete Sweeney endorses Mapex drums, Aquarian drum heads, Vic Firth drum sticks and Sabian cymbals. He can be contacted via E-mail at P9565@aol.

ACKNOWLEDGMENTS

I would like to thank Nat Gunod, Dave Smolover and Paula Abate at the National Guitar Workshop. Thanks also to: Neil Larrivee at Vic Firth; Bob Boos, Terry Shaw and Joe Healy at Sabian; Roy Burns and Chris Brady at Aquarian; and Chuck Turk and Jeff Ivester at Mapex. Thanks to my parents Patrick and Patricia Sweeney; my brother Paul; my niece Lacee; and my wife Robin. I would like to thank Dr. Tim Olsen for composing the songs and playing piano on the CD and Ryan Lucas for playing bass. Special thanks to Joe Morello for consenting to do the special three-part interview.

DEDICATION

I would like to dedicate this three-book series to the memory of the late, great baritone saxophonist Nick Brignola.

Track 1

A compact disc is available with each book of this series. Using these discs will help make learning more enjoyable and the information more meaningful. The CD will help you play the correct notes, rhythms and feel of each example. The track numbers below the symbols correspond directly to the example you want to hear. A CD symbol without a track number next to an example means that the example can be heard on the last CD track listed. Have fun!

INTRODUCTION

This is the first book in a three-part series intended to take you through the many contemporary styles and techniques of modern drumming. I sincerely hope you will enjoy this book and find the exercises and ideas useful. There are many challenging ideas and examples ahead, so be patient and work consistently. You'll be rewarded with excellent results.

You can use this book with the guidance of a teacher or for self study. It starts at the most basic level, beginning with reading drum music and fundamental snare drum technique. By the end of the book, you will be playing beats on the whole drumset and be ready to play in a band. You can then move on to the Intermediate and Mastering books to further develop your technique and musical knowledge.

The material in this book is intended to address important areas of a drummer's musical development, which I like to call the "Seven Cs."

1. **Concentration** — The ability to play or practice for many hours with *focus*. This is an absolute must for getting results and becoming a better player.
2. **Coordination** — The ability to perform different rhythms with the feet and hands, sometimes simultaneously.
3. **Consistency** — The ability to perform correctly on a consistent basis.
4. **Conception** — The ability to understand the big picture of music and how to better serve any given musical situation. Knowledge of reading music, understanding note values and awareness of various styles are all part of conception for the drummer.
5. **Composition** — The ability to *improvise* (instant composition) on the drumset. Includes the ability to understand various musical forms and structures.
6. **Creativity** — The ability to use one's musical imagination.
7. **Confidence** — The ability to perform anything with a high degree of certainty and assurance.

This series will give you tools in all of these areas. Good luck and have fun practicing. Let's get started!

THE DRUMSET

This is a very basic drumset. Some drumsets have several tom toms, two bass drums or other percussion instruments, such as a cowbell. Over time, your set will grow and change with your interests. Note that some of the exercises in this book call for two crash cymbals.

CHAPTER 1

Basic Terminology and Note Values

THE STAFF, MEASURES AND TIME SIGNATURES

THE STAFF

Music is written by placing *notes* on a *staff* of five lines and four spaces. The symbol at the beginning of the staff, which looks like two vertical lines, is called a *percussion clef*. The percussion clef tells you that the music on the staff is for drums. Each line and space represents a different instrument in the drumset.

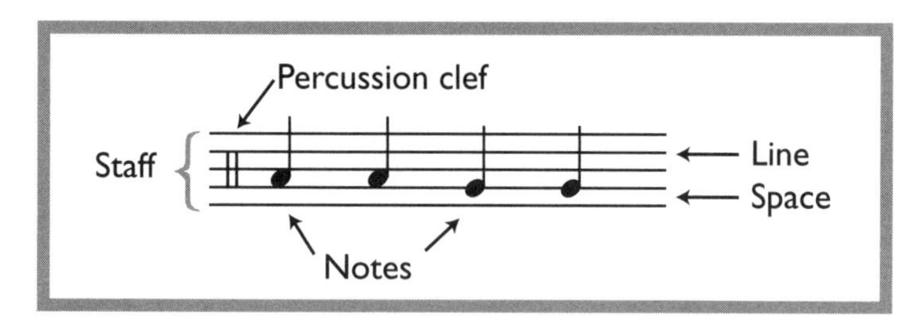

MEASURES

Beats, the most basic units of musical time, are grouped into *measures* of equal length—that is, each measure contains the same number of beats. Measures are marked with vertical *bar lines*. Short sections and excerpts end with a *double bar line*.

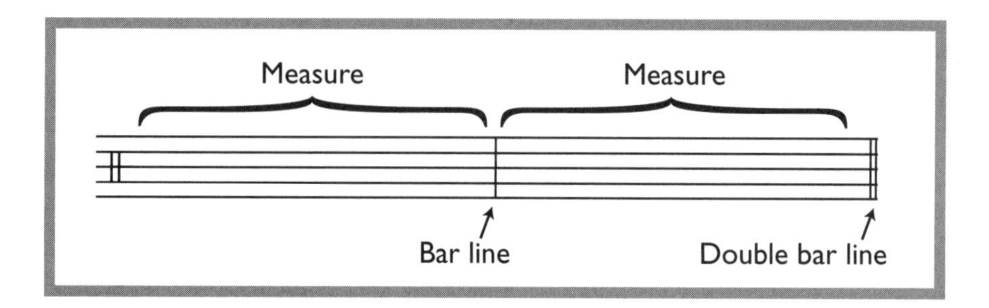

TIME SIGNATURES

At the beginning of every musical piece there is a *time signature*. A time signature tells you how to count the music. The top number tells you how many beats are in each measure; the bottom number tells you which kind of note (see "Note Values" on page 7) gets one beat. The most common time signature is $\frac{4}{4}$.

4 = Four beats per measure
4 = *Quarter note* ♩ gets one beat

NOTE VALUES

Now let's take a look at the different *note values* that are used in music.

WHOLE NOTE

The largest note value we cover is the *whole note*. A whole note lasts for four beats and it takes up a whole measure in $\frac{4}{4}$ time.

To accurately play a whole note, and all note values, you will need to count. To play a series of whole notes, count 1, 2, 3, 4 over and over while playing only beat one.

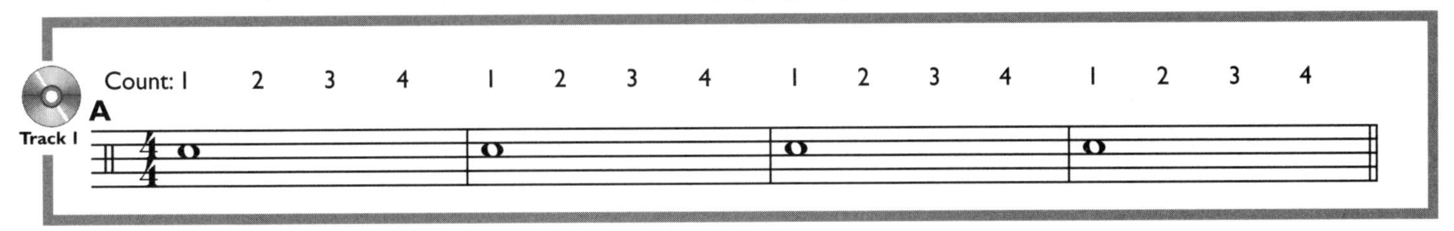

HALF NOTE

A *half note* lasts for two beats. The whole note is divided in half. To play a series of half notes, we play two evenly spaced notes in each measure. Count 1, 2, 3, 4 and play on beats 1 and 3.

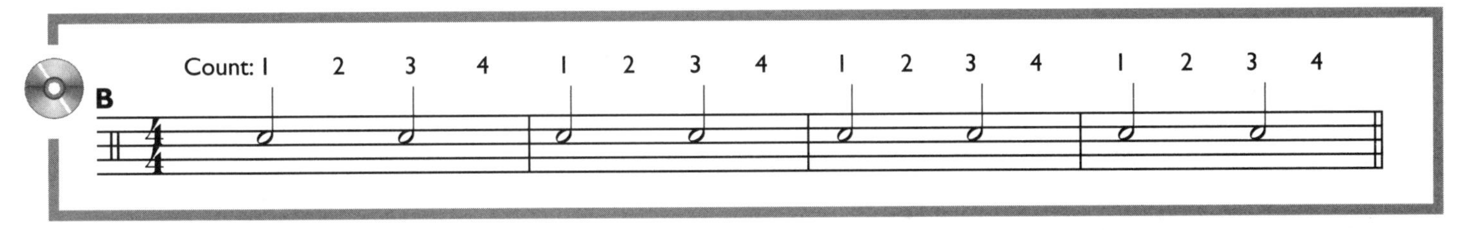

QUARTER NOTE

A *quarter note* lasts for one beat. The half note is divided in half, or you can think of the whole note being divided into four even quarters. To play a series of quarter notes, count 1, 2, 3, 4 and play on all four counts.

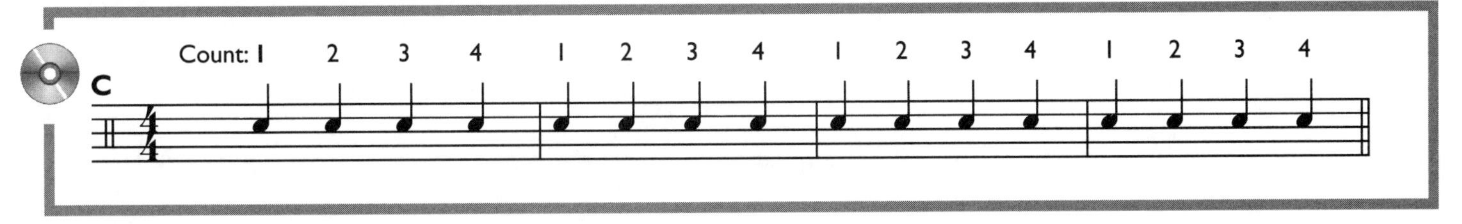

EIGHTH NOTE

When we divide quarter notes in half you get an even smaller note value called an *eighth note*. Eighth notes are easily recognized by the *flag*. Groups of eighth notes are attached by a heavy line called a *beam*.

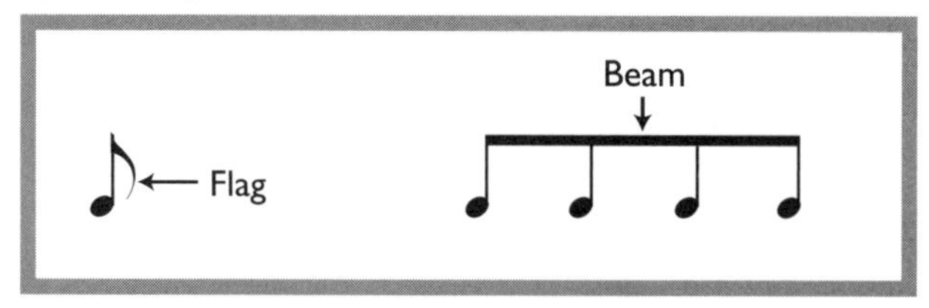

Count eighth notes 1–&*, 2–&, 3–&, 4–&.

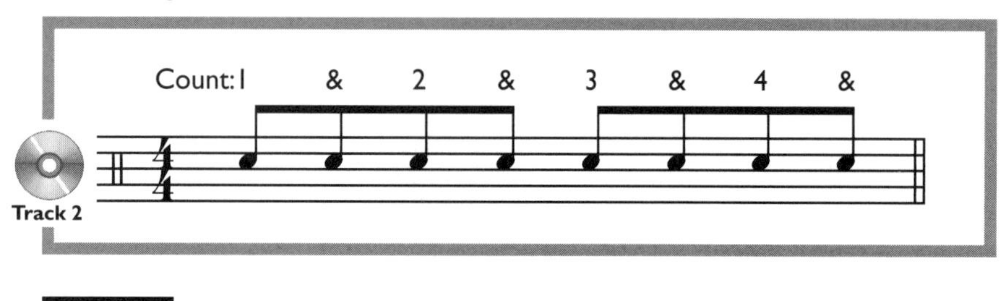

* = and

NOTE AND REST VALUE TABLES

Here are two charts to help you visualize the different note values we have just covered. Below the note values are the symbols for the corresponding *rests* for each note value. A rest indicates silence. When you come across a rest, simply stop playing for the value of the rest. Rests always remain part of the count, so be sure to give each one its full value.

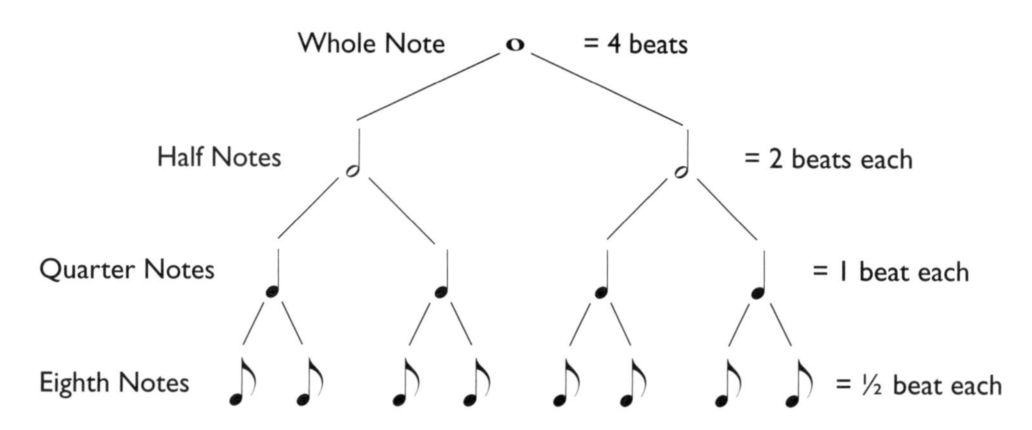

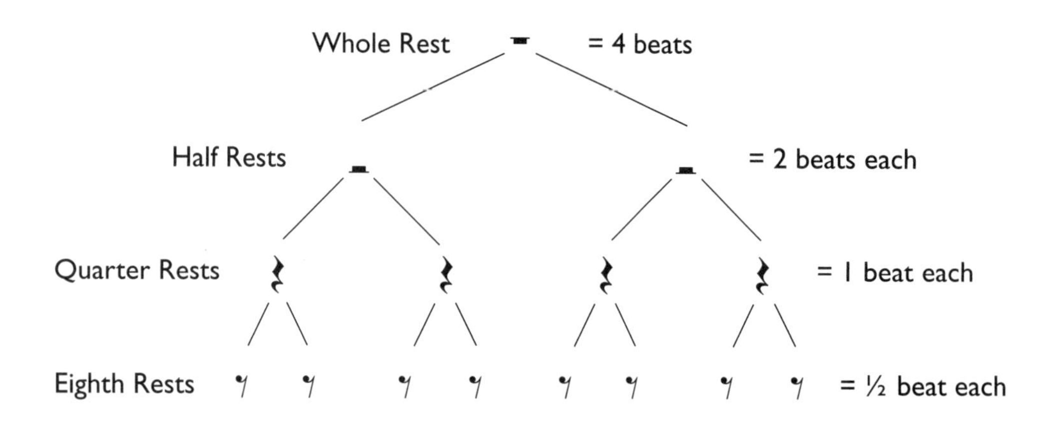

THE METRONOME AND READING EXERCISES

THE METRONOME

A *metronome* is an adjustable device used for measuring musical time. A metronome can help you keep steady, accurate time. It is especially useful for practicing because you can increase or decrease the *tempo* (speed).

The exercises in this book will have tempo markings expressed with numbers that you will find on your metronome. The numbers represent the number of beats per minute. In $\frac{4}{4}$, this tells us the speed of the quarter notes. For example: ♩ = 88.

These tempo markings are only suggestions. If you feel uncomfortable with an exercise, feel free to play it slower until you become more comfortable with it. Then increase the tempo bit by bit as you gain greater control.

READING EXERCISE NO. 1

The following reading exercise will make use of all of the note and rest values you have learned. Take your time and strive for accuracy. Be sure you count as you perform this exercise. On the CD that is available for this book, there will be a metronome playing along with the exercise on all four beats. This is referred to as a *click track*.

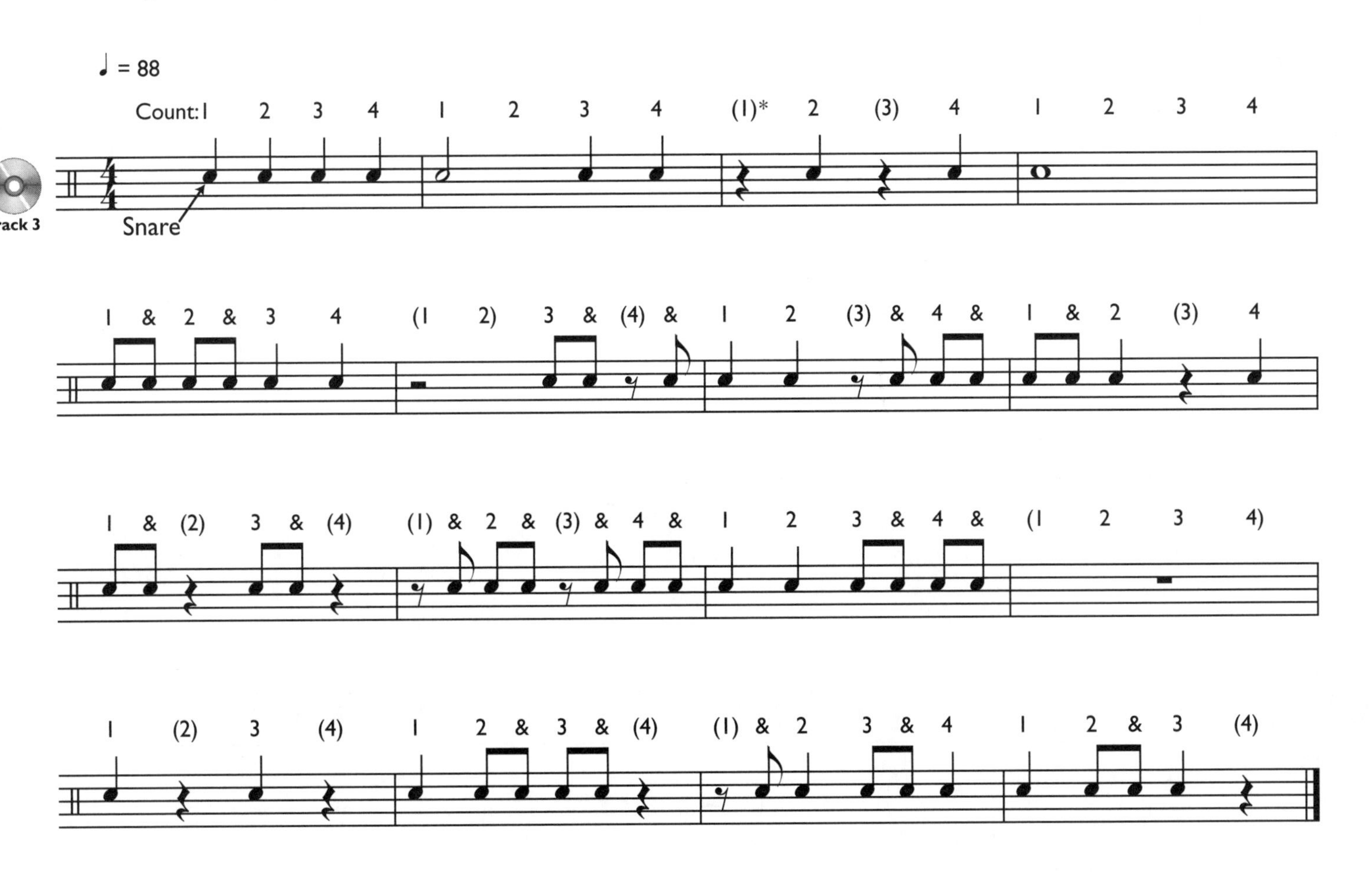

* Numbers in parentheses correspond to rests in music. They are used to assist in counting the beats.

THE REPEAT SIGN

A *repeat sign* is a way of saving space in written music. When you come to a repeat sign, go back to the beginning and play again from there.

Sometimes, only part of an exercise is repeated. When that happens, repeat signs surround the music to be repeated. When you come to the left-facing repeat (with dots on the left side), go back to the right-facing repeat (with dots on the right side) and play that section again. Then, if there is more music, continue past the left-facing repeat.

READING EXERCISE NO. 2

This exercise incorporates everything you have learned to this point. There are stickings indicated to tell you which hand should play which note.

R = Right hand
L = Left hand

If you are left-handed, simply reverse all of these stickings and start with the left hand. The counting is not written in the music, but as with Reading Exercise No. 1, count aloud as you play.

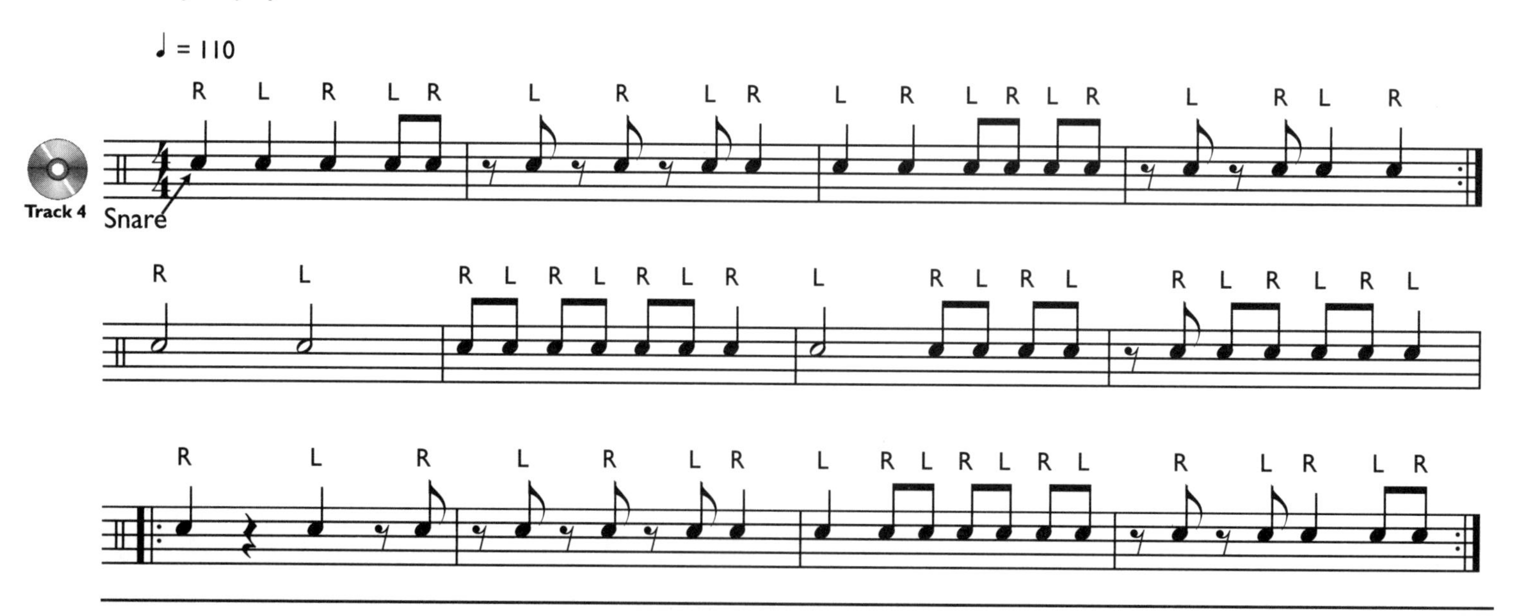

DRUMSET NOTATION

The following table will help you with the drumset notation used in this book. Drumset notation is very logical and visually easy to understand when you remember that all of the instruments appear on the staff the way the drumset is set up. In other words, the instruments appear on the staff according to their relative highness and lowness:

- The lower-pitched instruments like the bass drum appear on the lower lines and spaces;
- The higher-pitched instruments like the ride cymbal appear higher up on the staff. The stepped hi-hat, because it is played with the left foot, is the only exception to this rule.

Notice that the stems go up for instruments played with the hands, and down for instruments played with the feet.

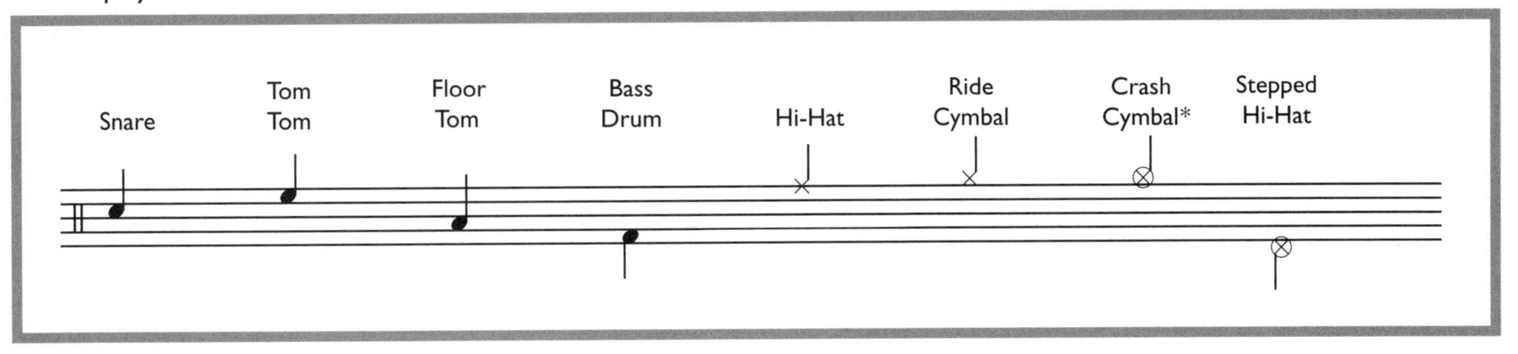

* It is a good idea to have two crash cymbals, and some of the exercises in this book call for two.

These are the symbols indicating the different sounds used when playing the hi-hat cymbals.

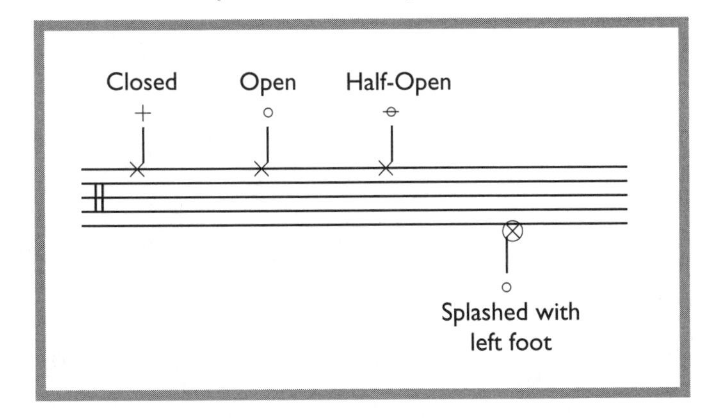

The notation for the various instruments of the drumset will be reviewed as needed throughout the book. Use this page as an easy, at-a-glance reference.

There is a photograph of the drumset on page 5.

CHAPTER 2

Snare Drum Technique

HOLDING THE STICKS

There are two ways of holding the sticks. Try both and find which one works for you.

MATCHED GRIP

Matched grip is a very natural and effective technique in which both hands hold the sticks the same way.

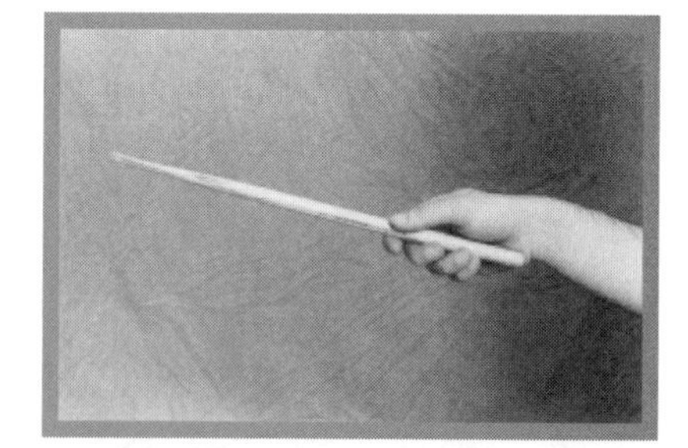

Grip the stick between the thumb and first joint of the index finger. Hold it about a third of the way, about five inches, up from the *butt*, which is the thickest end of the stick. Use the other three fingers to help control the stick.

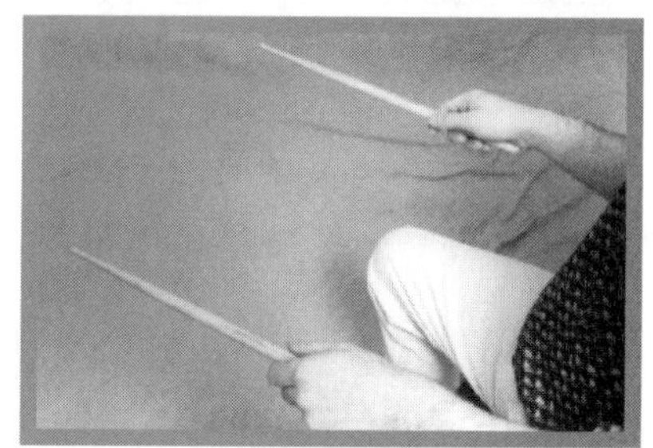

Make sure to avoid any unnecessary tension in the hand, using just enough to hold on to the stick. Keep a gap open between the thumb and first finger.

To play, turn the hand so that the back of the hand is facing upward. Think palm down.

TRADITIONAL GRIP

In the traditional grip, the right hand holds the stick as in the matched grip, while the left hand holds the stick in a sideways fashion as described below. (If you are left-handed, you may want to reverse these instructions.) This technique originated from military snare drumming in which the snare was slung around the neck and held to the side.

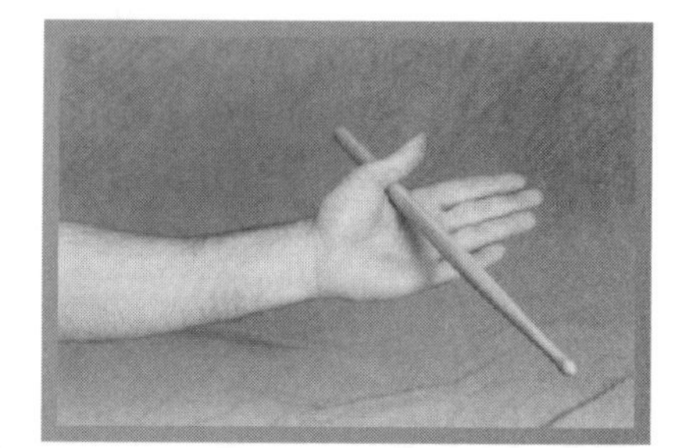

Step 1. Place the stick between the thumb and index finger, with one-third of the stick (the butt end) extending beyond the hand.

Step 2. The index and middle fingers should rest lightly on the top of the stick to act as a guide. The stick should rest across the top of the ring finger for support. The pinky should rest against the ring finger.

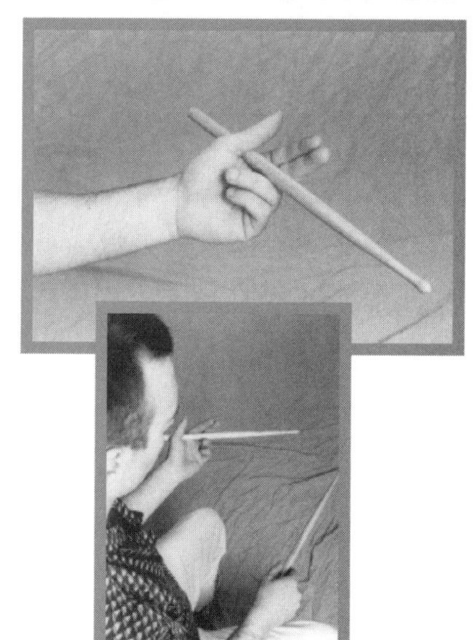

The right hand holds the stick matched grip, the left hand traditional grip.

BASIC STROKE TECHNIQUE

It is very important that your right-hand strokes sound the same as your left-hand strokes. Here are two suggestions for getting your hands to sound even.

1. Make sure that your hands begin their strokes from same height, and that they return to the same height. If one hand is higher than the other, they won't sound even.

Correct

Incorrect

2. Make sure both hands strike the drum with the same intensity.

Don't squeeze or pinch the sticks as you hit the drum. Any unnecessary tension will result in fatigue, cramping, or blisters. Let the stick do the work for you. Imagine the sticks like a basketball. When you throw a basketball down, it bounces back to you. The speed in which it returns is in direct relation to how much velocity was used in the initial throw. The same goes with your sticks. Allow your sticks to freely rebound so that you are more concerned with the initial "down" than the "up." The "up" will take care of itself because of the rebound. Try to avoid pressing or choking the stick into the head as you hit and you'll have great results!

As you play the snare drum, or any other drum in your set, strike the center of the head to achieve a full drum sound. Make sure that your strokes travel in a straight line directly down to the head. As you practice, watch your sticks so that you don't hit them together.

Correct.

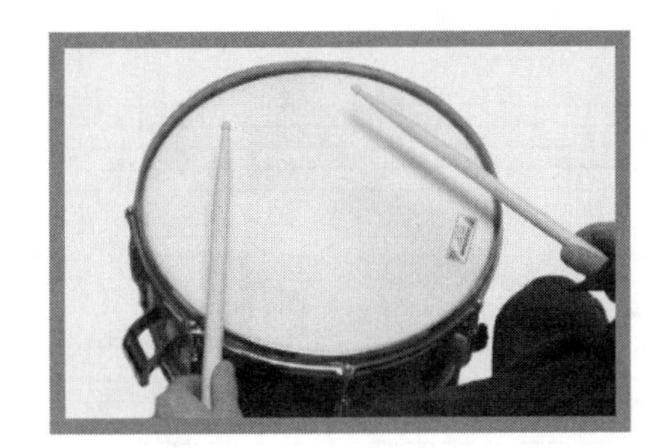

Incorrect.

RUDIMENT: SINGLE-STROKE ROLL

Rudiments are the basic vocabulary of the drums. They were created many years ago by the military snare drummers and are essential for developing your hand technique. The first rudiment we'll work on is the *single-stroke roll*. The single-stroke roll uses one stroke per hand: R–L–R–L (left-handed drummers can reverse the sticking L–R–L–R). Start slowly and work on the evenness of the roll. Don't be in a hurry to play fast! Speed comes later, when the technique is executed evenly on a consistent basis.

SINGLE-STROKE ROLL IN QUARTER NOTES

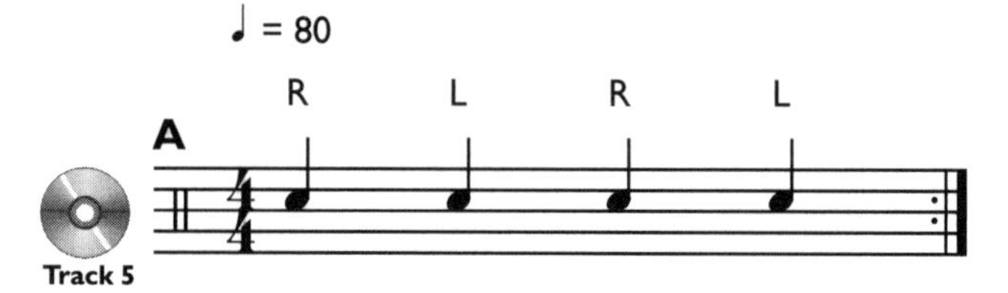

SINGLE-STROKE ROLL IN EIGHTH NOTES

SINGLE-STROKE ROLL PLAYED IN DIFFERENT NOTE VALUES

Make sure to count and listen for consistency. Don't play too quickly at first; walk before you run!

RUDIMENT: DOUBLE-STROKE ROLL

The next rudiment will be the *double-stroke roll.* This has two even strokes per hand: R–R–L–L.

DOUBLE-STROKE ROLL IN QUARTER NOTES

DOUBLE-STROKE ROLL IN EIGHTH NOTES

Remember to keep the sticks at an even height and allow them to rebound as you play. With practice this will ensure an even-sounding roll.

SINGLE- AND DOUBLE-STROKE ROLL COMBINATIONS

The following exercises are combinations of single- and double-stroke rolls. All drumming is based on combinations of these two rolls, so it is necessary to practice the transition from one roll to the other. Take your time and strive for an even sound.

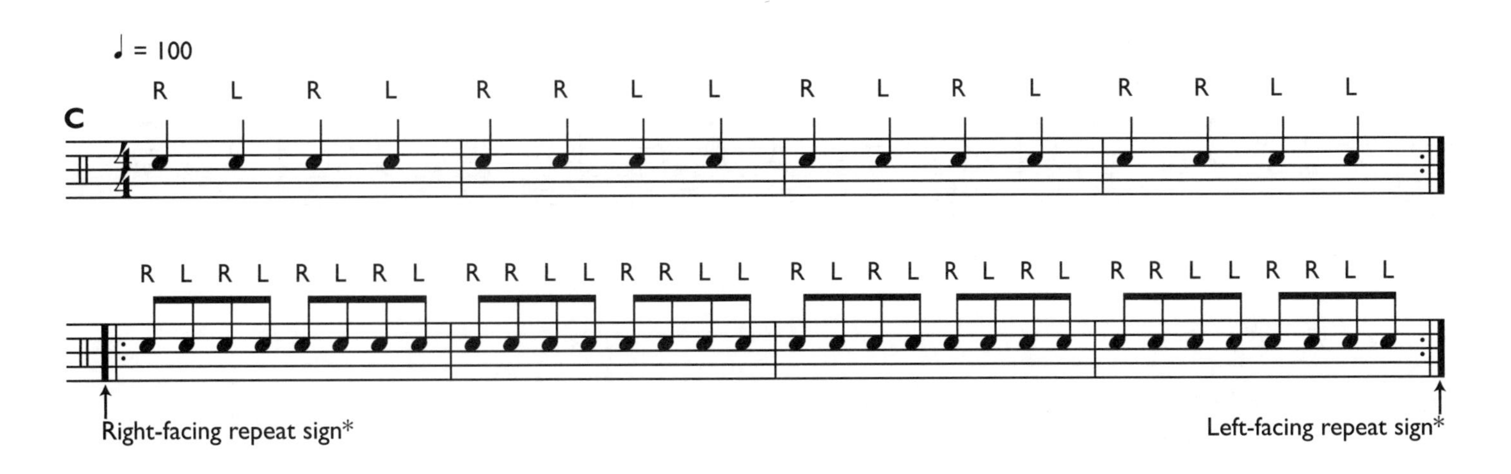

* When you reach the left-facing repeat sign, come back to the most recent right-facing repeat sign and play the music between the repeat signs again.

RUDIMENT: THE PARADIDDLE

Our next rudiment will be the *paradiddle*. The paradiddle is a combination of single- and double-stroke rolls. The sticking is R–L–R–R, L–R–L–L. When the military snare drummers of many years ago were in the field, they had no written music so they devised terminology that could easily describe the different rudiments verbally. Think of it this way: "pa" is a single stroke, "ra" is a single stroke and "did-dle" is a double stroke.

PARADIDDLE IN QUARTER NOTES

PARADIDDLE IN EIGHTH NOTES

Here are some other stickings for the paradiddle. Make sure you memorize each sticking and that they flow evenly from one to the other.

SHORT-ROLL COMBINATIONS

The following rudiments are short rolls using the double-stroke roll. All of these rolls should be practiced starting and ending with both the right and left hands. Each roll should be practiced individually, then one after the other to make a nice workout routine.

THREE-STROKE ROLL

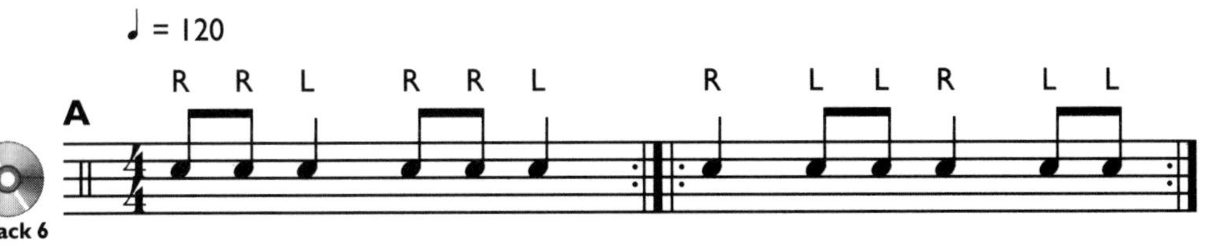

FIVE-STROKE ROLL

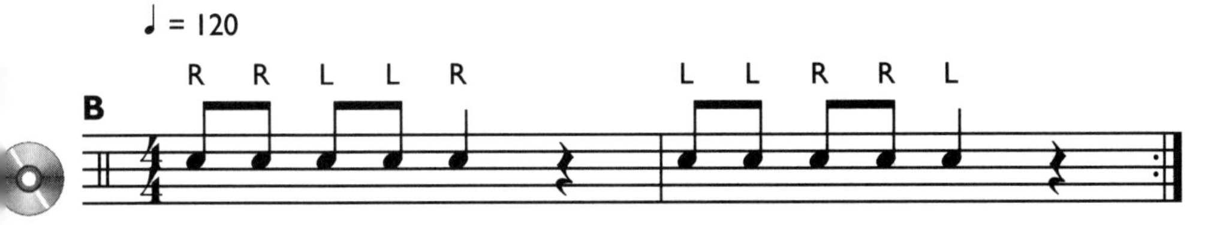

SIX-STROKE ROLL

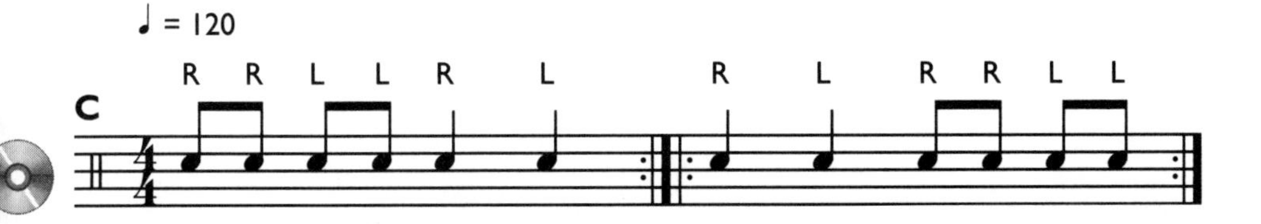

SEVEN-STROKE ROLL

NINE-STROKE ROLL

TEN-STROKE ROLL

ELEVEN-STROKE ROLL

THIRTEEN-STROKE ROLL

FIFTEEN-STROKE ROLL

SNARE DRUM SOLO

After practicing your rudiments, you're now ready for a solo piece. Practice slowly at first and observe all of the stickings. Have fun!

♩ = 140 200

Track 8

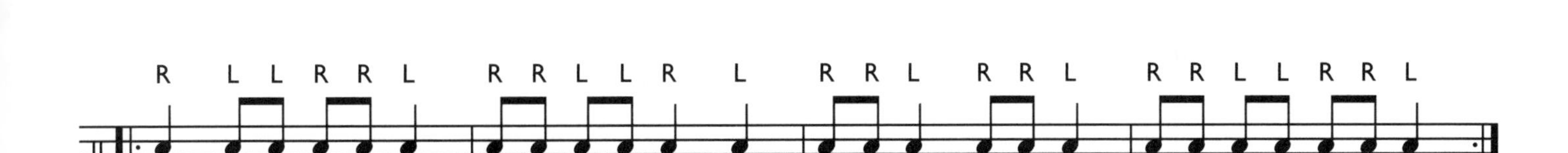

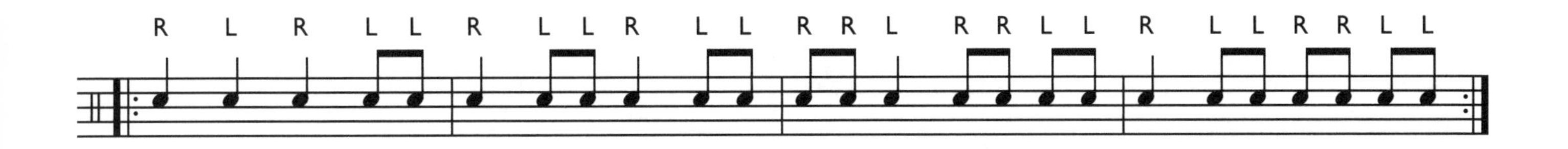

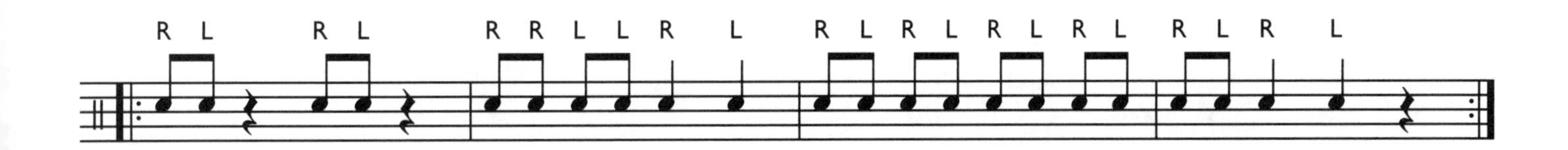

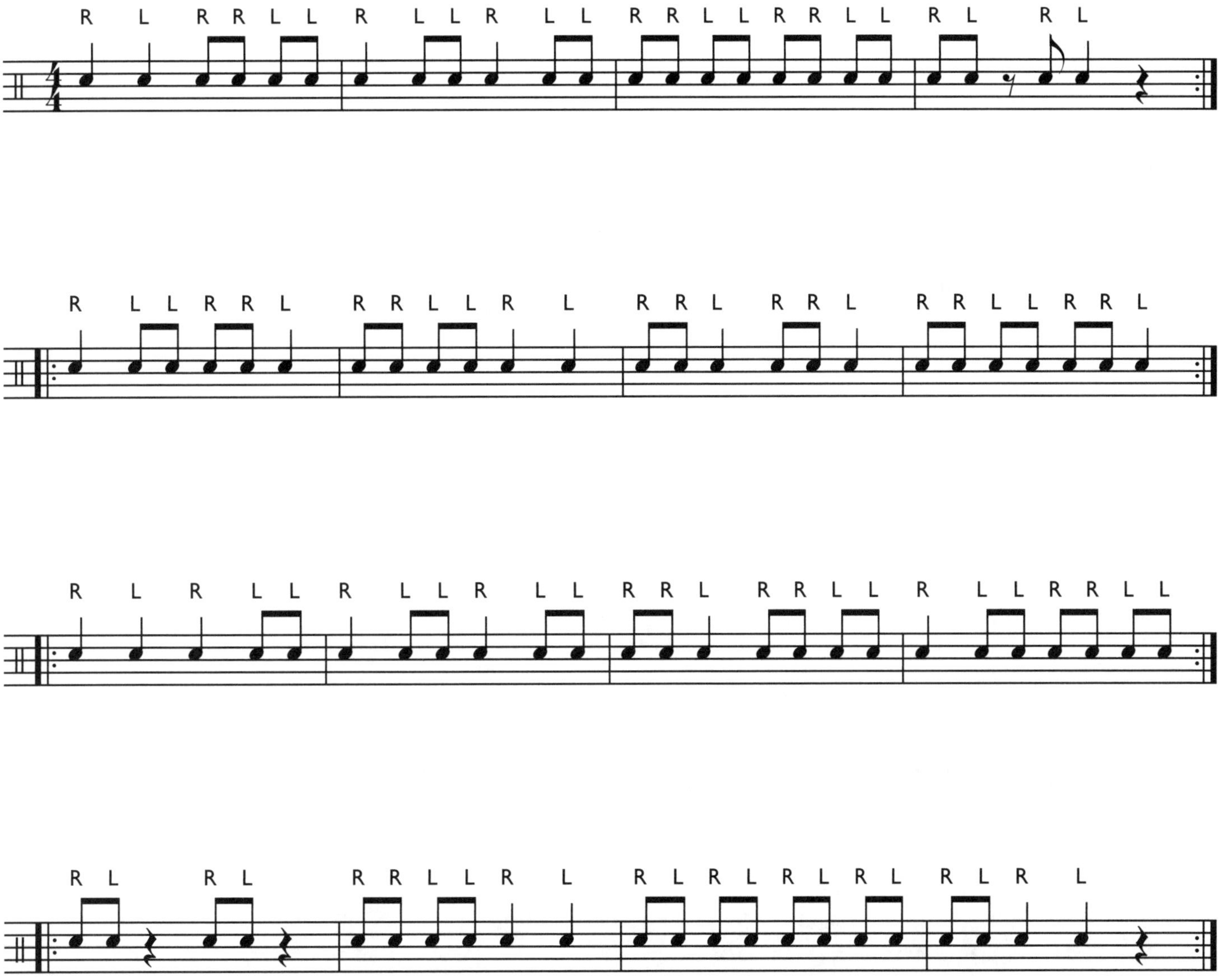
R L R R L L R L L R L L R R L L R R L L R L R L
R L L R R L R R L L R L R R L R R L R R L L R R L
R L R L L R L L R L L R R L R R L L R L L R R L L
R L R L R R L L R L R L R L R L R L R L R L

CHAPTER 3

Accent Studies and Dynamics

To *accent* is to emphasize (play louder) a note. Accents are very important and are frequently used to create interest and contrast. They are also tremendously useful for building your facility on the drums.

When performing passages with accents, it is important to remember that a definite contrast between accented and unaccented strokes will sound better and communicate to the listener more effectively. Let's look at the different types of stick motions and stick positions involved in effectively executing accented and non-accented notes.

FOUR BASIC MOVEMENTS

THE FULL STROKE

The *full stroke* will begin with the tip pointed at the ceiling (at a 90 degree angle to the floor). Throw the stick down and strike the drum. Allow the stick to freely rebound back to the starting 90 degree position. This is for an accented stroke followed by another accented stroke.

DOWN STROKE

The *down stroke* begins in the same position as the full stroke. Bring the stick down and strike the drum, but now stop the rebound of the stick approximately one inch from the drum head rather than letting it bounce back. This is for an accented stroke followed by an unaccented stroke.

THE TAP STROKE

The *tap stroke* is an unaccented note. The stroke is played from about one to two inches above the drum head. This stroke is for an unaccented note followed by another unaccented note.

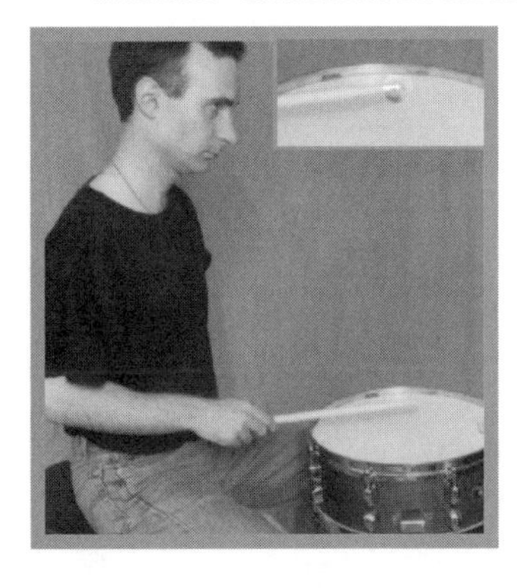
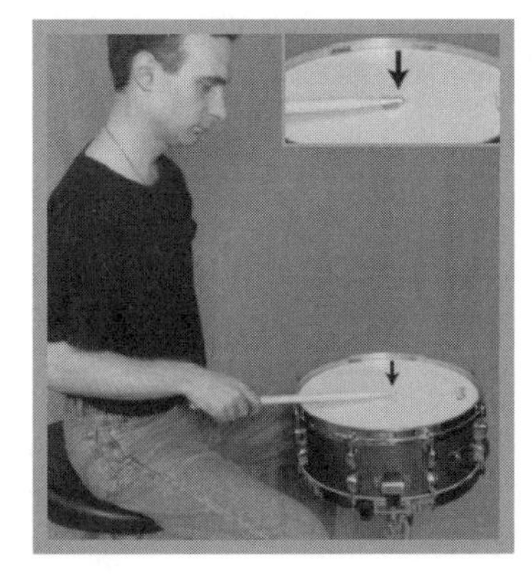

THE TAP/UP STROKE

This stroke begins as a tap but is followed by bringing the stick back to the 90 degree position, where the full stroke began. This is for an unaccented note followed by an accented note.

COMBINATION EXERCISE

Let's put all of the four movements into practice with this accent exercise. This symbol > indicates the note should be accented.

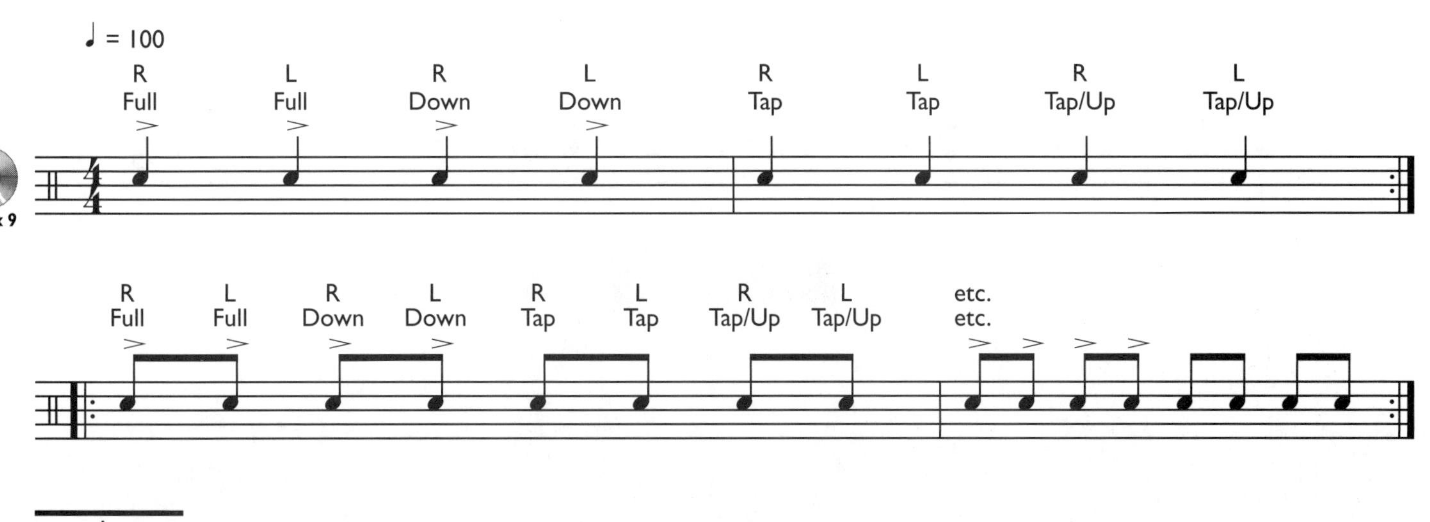

> = Accent

COMBINATION STUDIES

The following accent study will make use of the four basic movements covered on pages 20 and 21. They will be indicated by the following abbreviations:

F = Full stroke
D = Down stroke
T = Tap stroke
T/U = Tap/up stroke

Be sure to count so you can accurately place all of the accents. Don't squeeze or pinch the stick as you hit harder for the accented notes. Remember that the height of the stick will naturally make the sound of the stroke louder or softer.

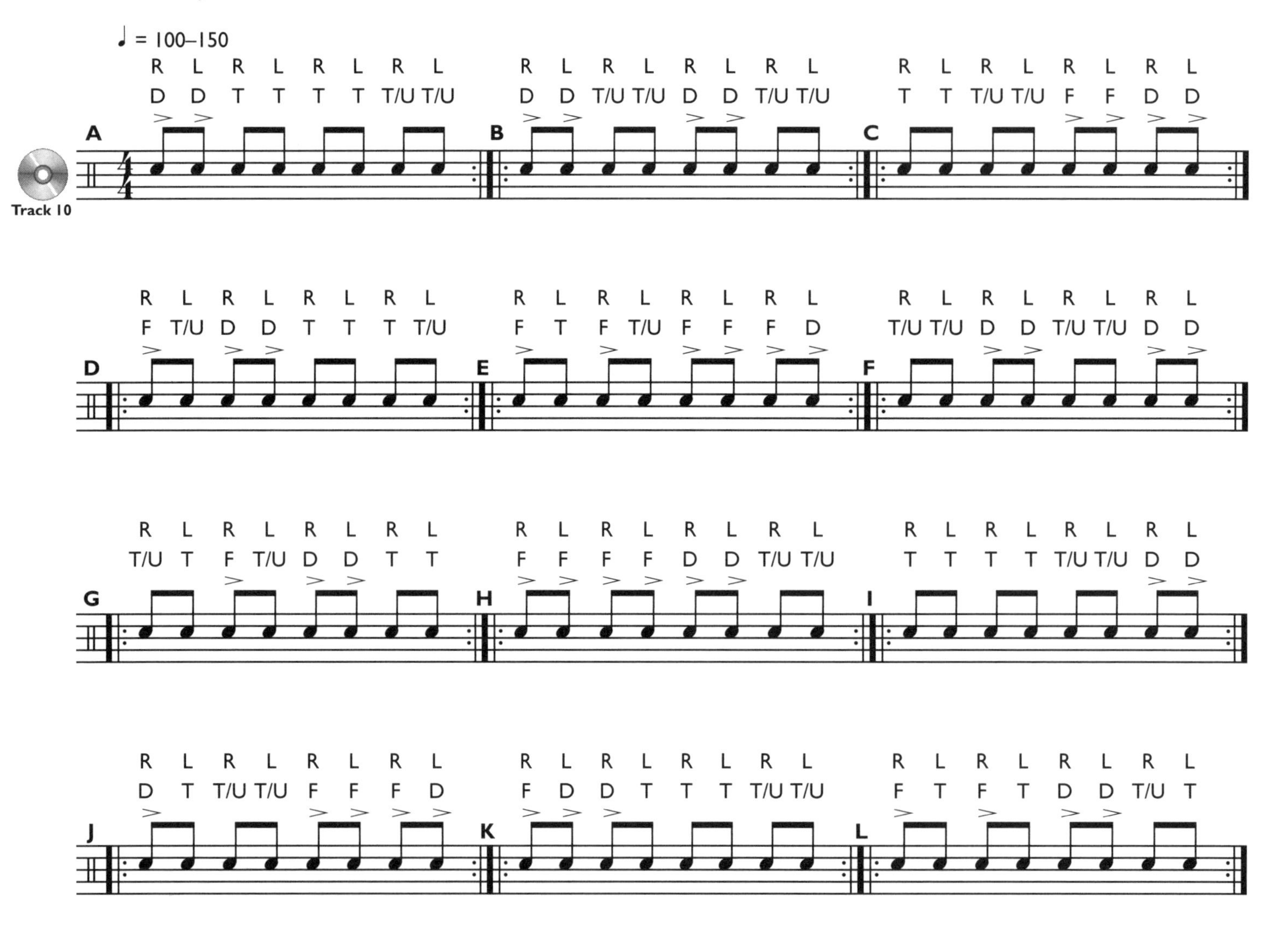

SINGLE EIGHTH-NOTE ACCENTS

The following exercises will give you accent control within the single-stroke roll in eighth notes. These are building blocks you will need in order to be able to play interesting drum fills and solos. This exercise works on all eight of the possible points within a measure of eighth notes that an accent can fall. Be sure to count as you play these exercises.

TWO EIGHTH-NOTE ACCENTS

Let's take the accent idea a little further and play two accents in a row throughout a single-stroke roll. Think of the accents as a melody line and the unaccented notes as support underneath.

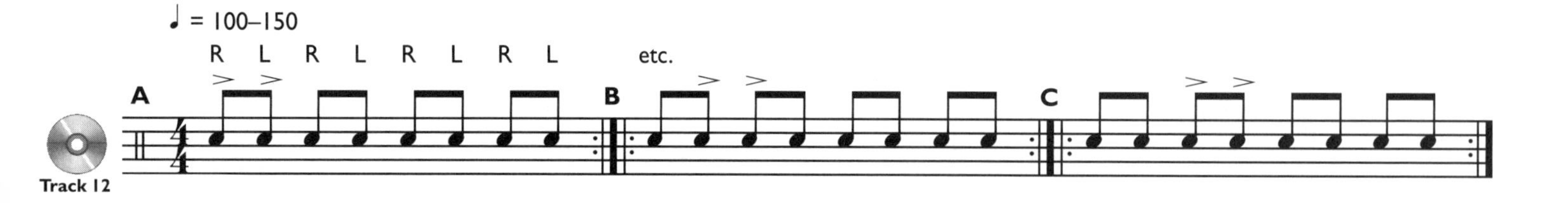

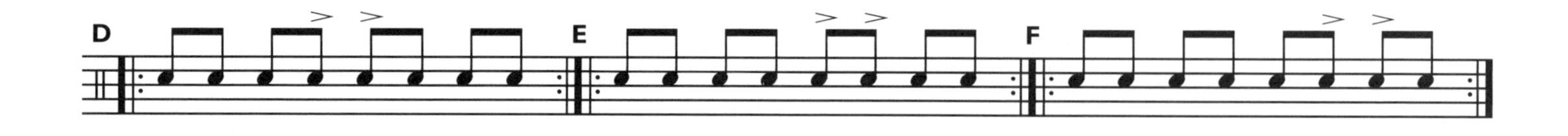

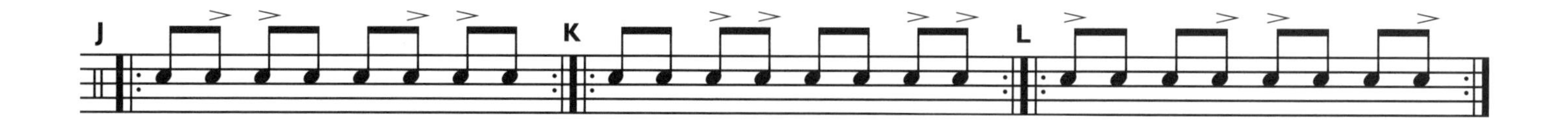

PROGRESSIVE EIGHTH-NOTE ACCENTS

In this series of exercises we will take the accenting concept a step further and progressively add an accented note each measure. This is a very effective way to improve your control of the single-stroke roll. Practice slowly and evenly, then take it faster as you become more familiar with the workout.

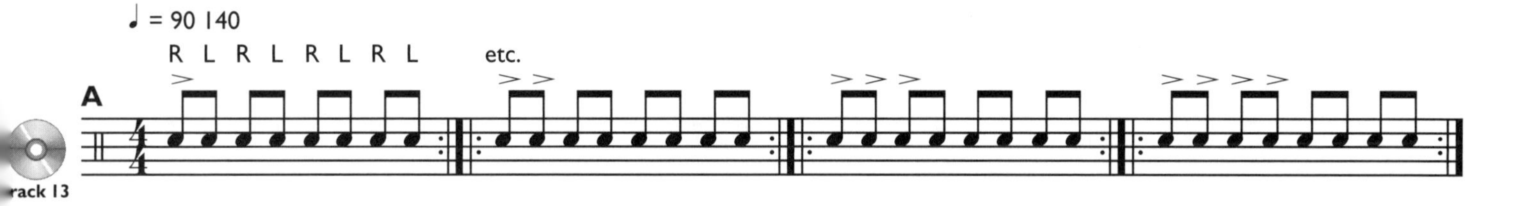

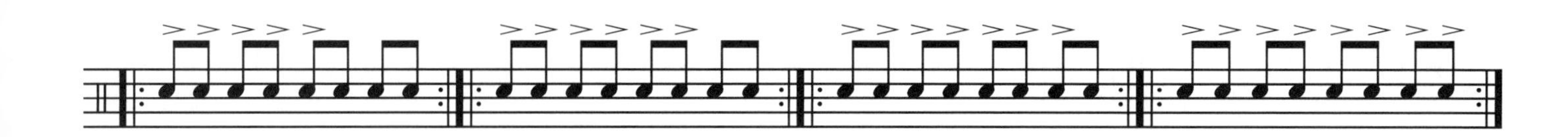

This exercise has one measure without accents and one measure with accents.

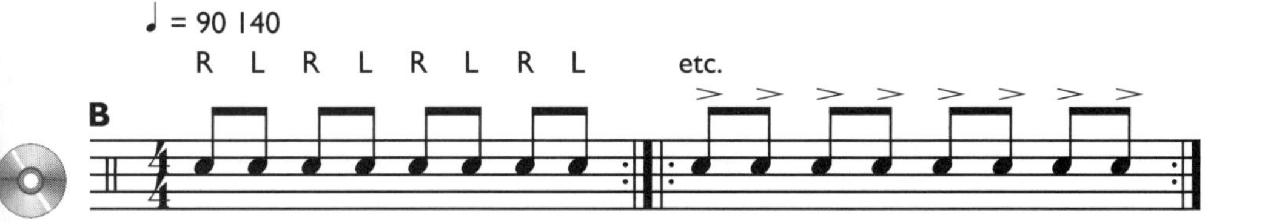

ACCENTING THE DOUBLE-STROKE ROLL

The double-stroke roll can sound uneven at first because there is a tendency to over-emphasize the first note of each double. The following exercises will focus on accenting the double-stroke roll, especially the often neglected second note. This will be a challenge at first, so take your time and be patient. The pay-off will be a great sounding double-stroke roll!

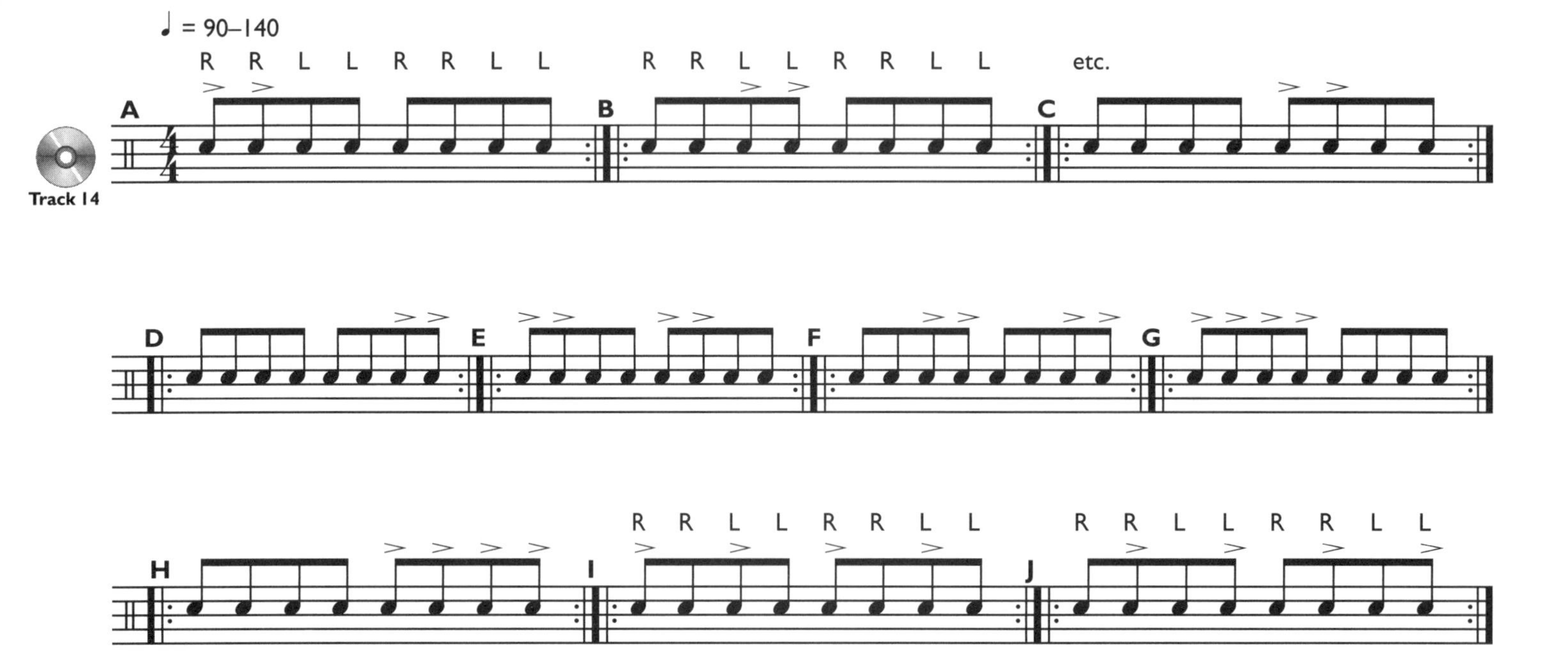

PHOTO • JEFFREY MAYER/COURTESY OF STAR FILE PHOTO, INC.

***Ginger Baker** was the drummer for the 1960s British rock group Cream, which also included bassist Jack Bruce and guitarist Eric Clapton. Cream defined the power-trio approach to rock music and pushed the envelope in rock improvisation. Baker's fiery extended solos were a high-light of their concerts.*

DYNAMICS

Dynamics are changes in *volume* (degree of loudness or softness). Like accents, these dynamic changes create interest and contrast for the listener. *Dynamic markings* are used in written music to indicate these changes in volume. Here's a list of the dynamic markings you are most likely to encounter and their Italian (the universal musical language) names.

Symbol	Italian Name	Description
fff	*fortississimo*	Extremely loud
ff	*fortissimo*	Very loud
f	*forte*	Loud
mf	*mezzo-forte*	Moderately loud
mp	*mezzo-piano*	Moderately soft
p	*piano*	Soft
pp	*pianissimo*	Very soft
ppp	*pianississimo*	Extremely soft

DYNAMICS EXERCISE

The following exercise will help develop your ability to quickly change dynamic levels while playing the single-stroke roll.

♩ = 100

rack 15

Dynamic markings such as these will only be seen in classical music. You should, however, always bear in mind that varying dynamics is a musical option.

Now that you've worked on accenting the single-stroke roll, it's time to have fun and play some one- and two-measure combinations. These ideas will just get you started. You should continue on and create patterns of your own.

ONE-MEASURE ACCENT PATTERNS

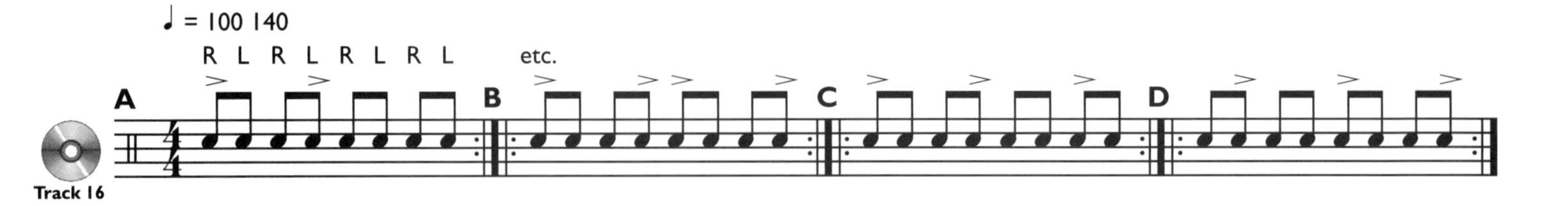

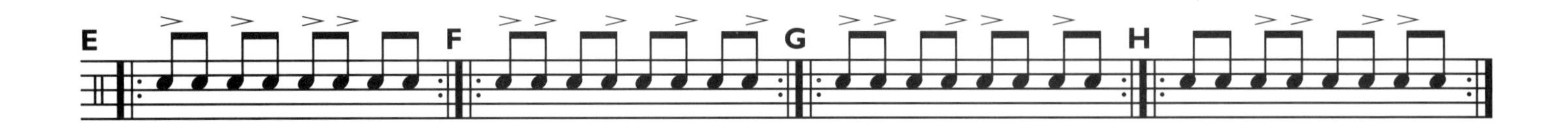

TWO-MEASURE ACCENT PATTERNS

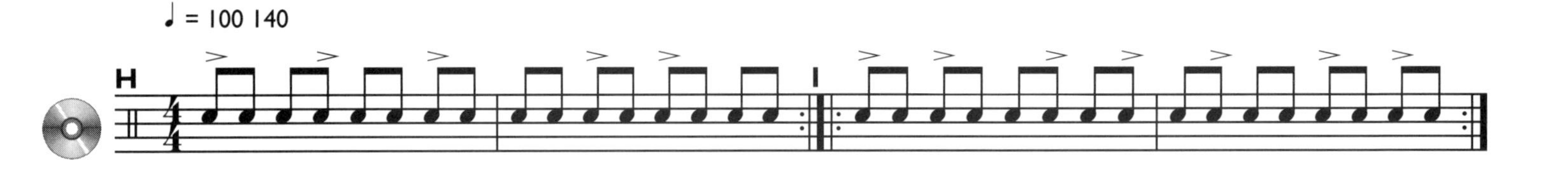

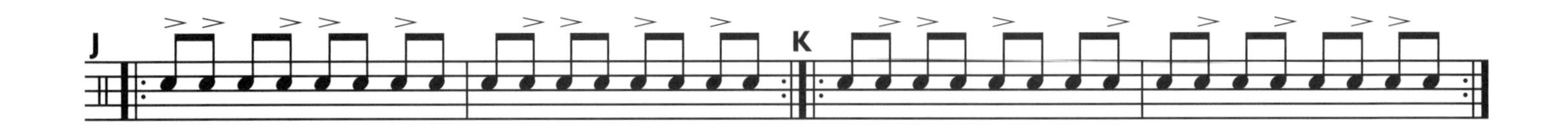

CHAPTER 4

Basic Drumset Coordination: Rock Beats

In this chapter, you will learn about the basic coordination involved with playing eighth-note rock beats on the drumset. Let's get started with the bass drum.

THE BASS DRUM

To get started, let's play steady quarter notes on the bass drum.

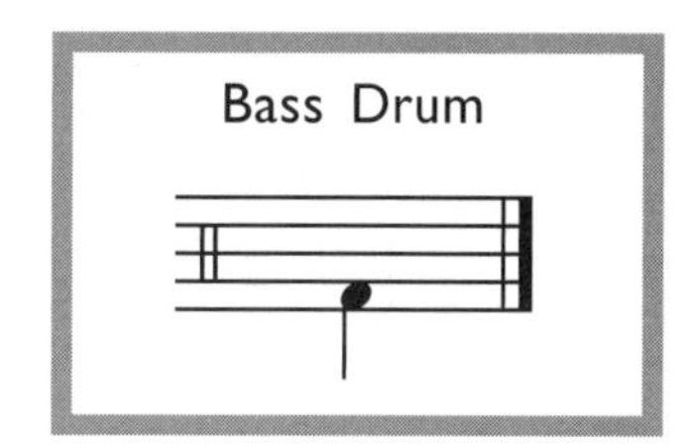

BASS DRUM TECHNIQUE

There are two basic ways to play the bass drum.

1. **Heel-down or flat-footed.** With this technique you play the bass drum pedal (right foot) with your entire foot flat on the pedal board. This technique is great for feeling balanced at the set and for being able to control the *beater* (the part of the bass drum pedal that hits the drum head) at low dynamic levels.

2. **Heel-up.** With this technique you play the bass drum with your heel raised and the toes and front part of your foot on the *footboard* (the part of the pedal where the foot rests). This is great when you want to play louder because you use the whole leg.

Practice both techniques.

EXERCISES FOR PLAYING THE BASS DRUM

These exercises will get you comfortable with playing the bass drum. Make sure that your strokes are even—they should all sound the same— and that the time is steady. This will be especially important when you begin to play drum beats using the whole drumset. Try using both the heel-up and heel-down methods.

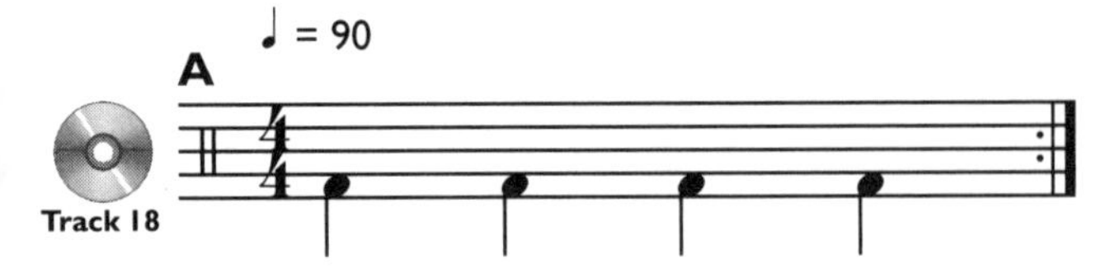

THE HI-HAT

The next step is to move to the hi-hat. Your left foot should be on the hi-hat pedal, which makes the top cymbal come down and hit the bottom cymbal. The hi-hat is a very important element of drumset playing, and can be used for many different sounds. You can get a very "trashy" sound by leaving them open as you hit them with your sticks or a very tight sound by leaving them closed. Or, you can play the hi-hat cymbals with your foot. As with the bass drum, there are two ways to play the hi-hats with your foot.

1. Heel-down

2. Heel-up

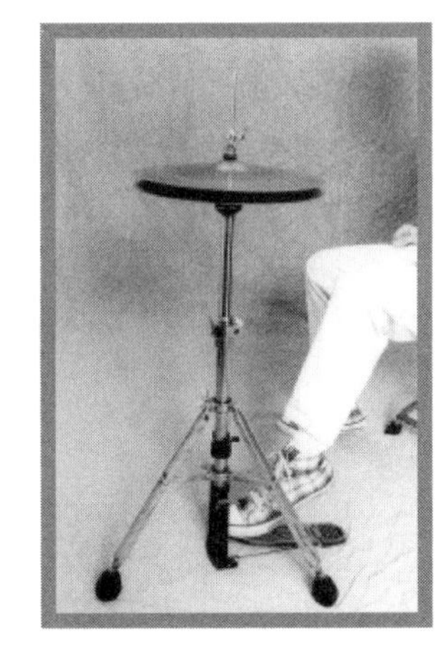

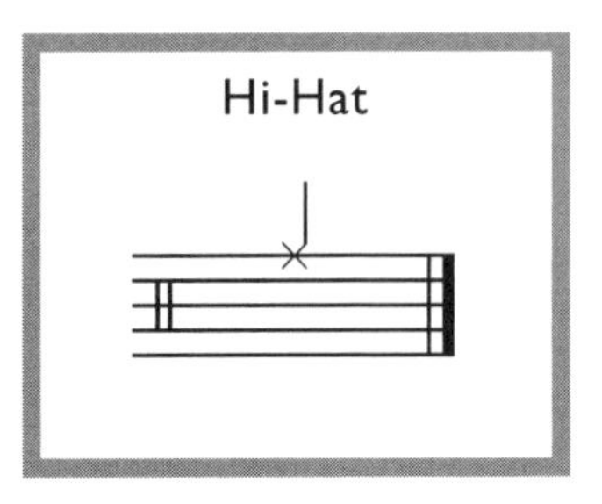

EXERCISES FOR PLAYING THE HI-HAT

To get started playing the hi-hat, take your right hand and cross it over your left. Press down the hi-hat pedal with your left foot to close the top hi-hat cymbal. Take some time to experiment with how much tension you need to keep the hi-hats closed. Let's play steady quarter notes on the closed hi-hat with the right hand.

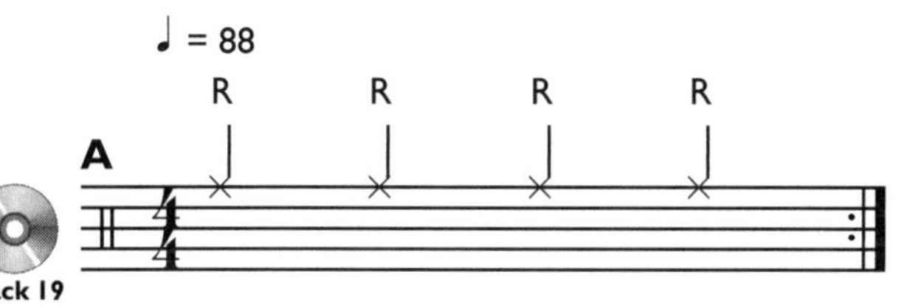

Now switch to eighth notes.

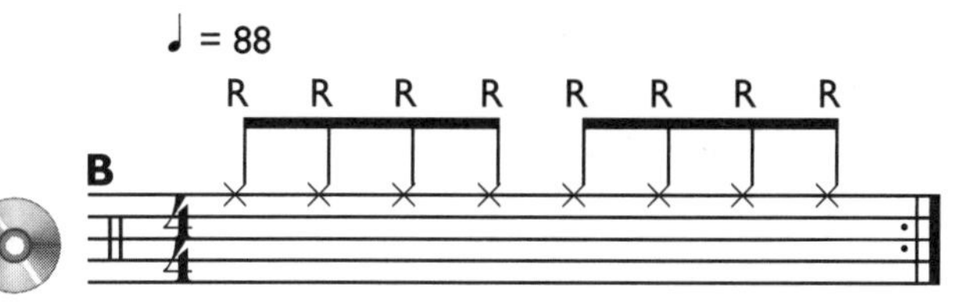

Here is your first exercise combining two different instruments of the drumset. Play quarter notes on the bass drum and eighths on the hi-hat. It is very important that your bass drum beat is steady.

♩ = 88

C

Turn the page to prepare to play three instruments at once: the bass drum, hi-hat and snare drum!

SNARE, BASS DRUM AND HI-HAT ROCK BEATS

QUARTER NOTE HI-HAT

Let's begin by playing quarter notes on the hi-hat (right hand) and bass drum. This should be very natural because the right hand and foot are playing in *unison* (together).

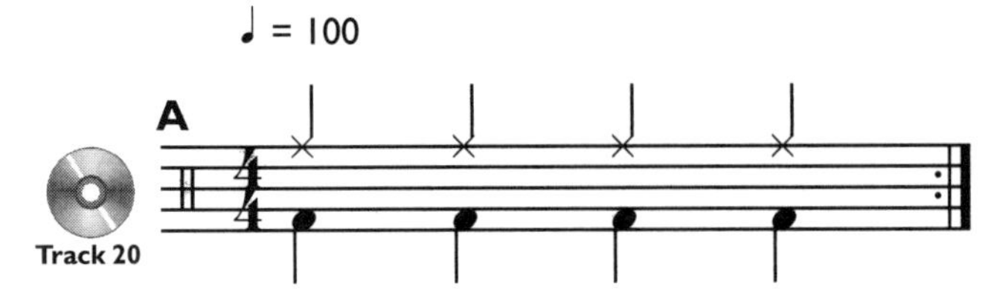

When you are comfortable playing the hi-hat and bass drum in unison, add the snare drum on beats 2 and 4 with the left hand. Notice how the coordination works between the feet and hands. Beats 1 and 3 are unison with the hi-hat and bass drum, while beats 2 and 4 are unison with the hi-hat, snare and bass drum.

♩ = 100

B

Now let's play the bass drum only on beats 1 and 3. Repeat this until you can perform it easily and consistently.

Although he is known for being the drummer for The Rolling Stones, jazz is ***Charlie Watts'*** *first love. In the 1980s he toured worldwide with a huge big band that included many of England's top musicians. In 1991, he organized a bop quintet that paid tribute to Charlie Parker.*

PHOTO • BARRIE WENTZELL\COURTESY OF STAR FILE, INC.

EIGHTH-NOTE ROCK BEATS WITH QUARTER-NOTE BASS-DRUM VARIATIONS

When you feel confident playing quarter notes on the hi-hat, it's time to move on to eighth notes. The following series of exercises will help you put the bass drum on any quarter note in a measure of $\frac{4}{4}$ time. Take your time and be sure to count as you perform these exercises.

When these variations are comfortable, go ahead and work the tempo up a little faster. Make sure you can play them consistently and accurately.

SYNCOPATED BEATS

Syncopation means to shift the emphasis to the "weak" beat or offbeat. Consider this beat:

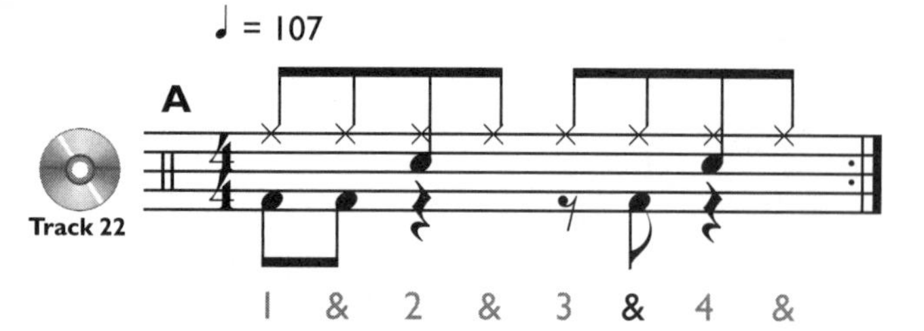

If you move the snare hit on beat 2 to the "& of 2," you have syncopation. The weaker part of the beat, the offbeat (the "& of 2"), is now emphasized rather than the first part of beat 2, the stronger beat, which we'll call the *onbeat*. Many of the hits of James Brown are based on this kind of syncopation.

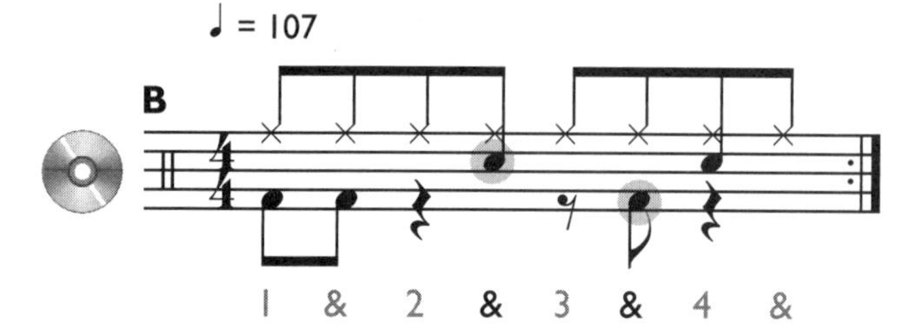

Here are some examples to check out.

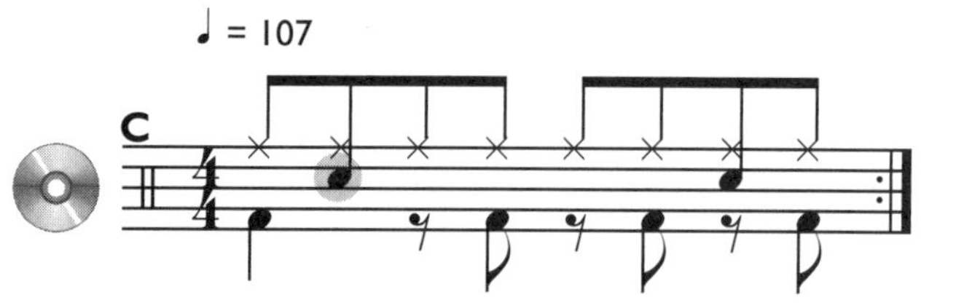

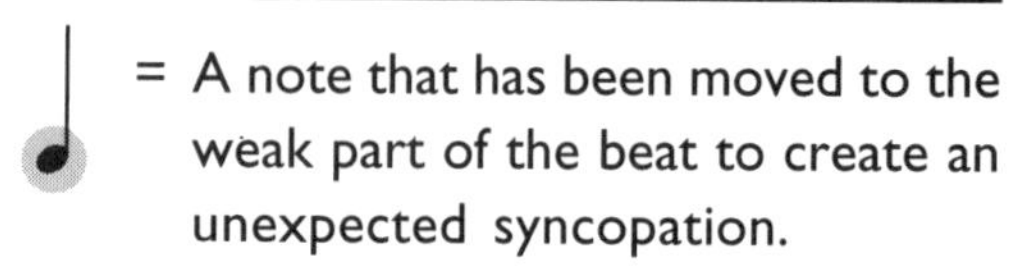

***Ringo Starr**, born Richard Starkey, was the drummer in the Beatles from 1962 to 1970 and thus one of the most famous musicians of the 1960s.*

PHOTO • MICHAEL BRITO\STAR FILES, INC.

EIGHTH-NOTE BEATS WITH SINGLE EIGHTH-NOTE BASS-DRUM VARIATIONS

The following exercises will expand your ability to place a single eighth note on any one of the eight different places an eighth note can occur in a measure of $\frac{4}{4}$. The ability to place the bass drum in any of these spots is necessary in order to play more difficult and complex grooves.

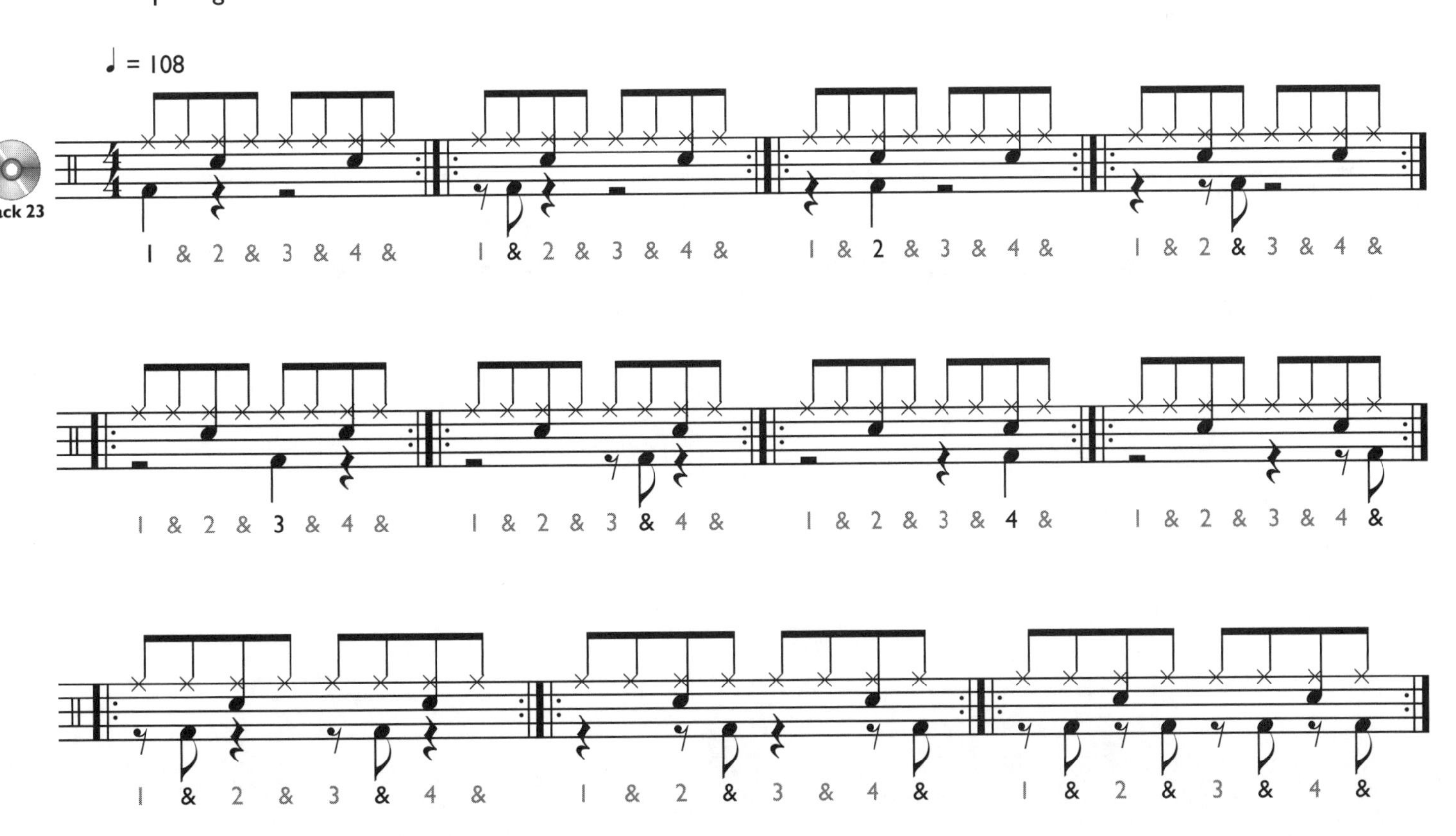

EIGHTH-NOTE BEATS WITH TWO CONSECUTIVE NOTES IN THE BASS DRUM

The next step will be to work on beats that have two consecutive eighth notes on the bass drum. As you practice these grooves, make sure the eighth notes on the bass drum both sound the same. Take your time and work on each of these beats to the point where they consistently sound great.

MIXED BASS DRUM COMBINATIONS

Now we're ready to combine the single- and double-note bass-drum ideas you've worked on. Many of these beats originated from popular songs from bands such as Led Zeppelin, AC/DC and The Beatles. These beats sound great if they are played in a solid, convincing manner. It's all in the attitude!

CHANGING THE HI-HAT SOUND

There are many ways to change the sound of the hi-hats as you are playing a rock beat. The easiest way is to leave the top cymbal half open. You can do this by slightly letting up on the tension with your left foot on the pedal. Listen to the song "Rock and Roll" by Led Zeppelin (John Bonham on drums) for some inspiration. Here are some examples.

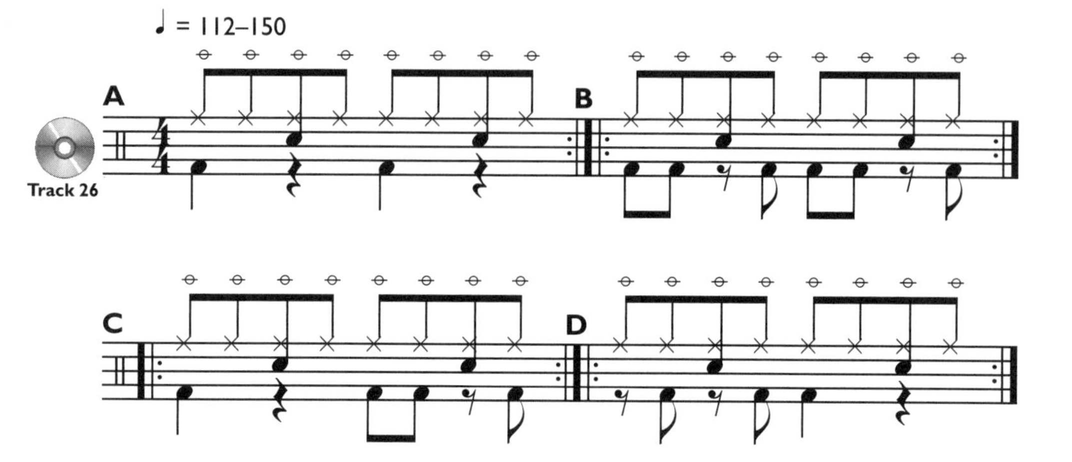

Another way to play closed hi-hat eighth notes is to accent quarter notes (every other eighth note). This will really help define the pulse as you are playing a beat.

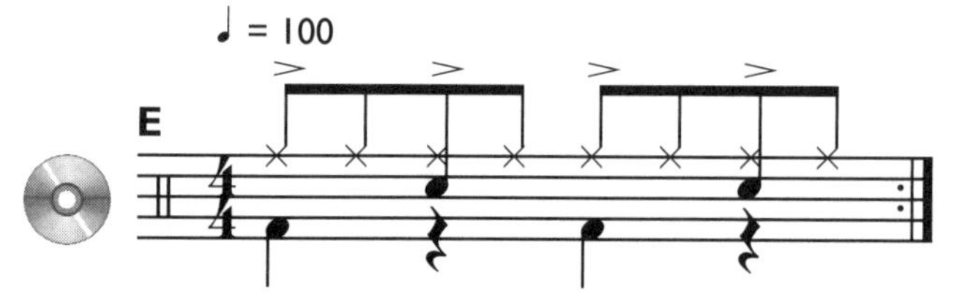

Here's an example of accenting all of the *offbeats* (the "&"s) on the hi-hat.

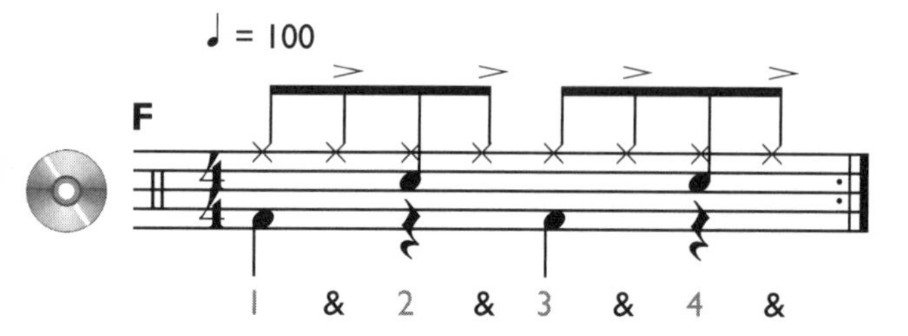

OPEN AND CLOSING THE HI-HATS

A great way to vary the sound of a beat is to open and close the top cymbal as you play eighth notes. This is achieved by taking the left foot and moving it forward and backward on the pedal as you play. Let's get started by first working on the hi-hat part by itself.

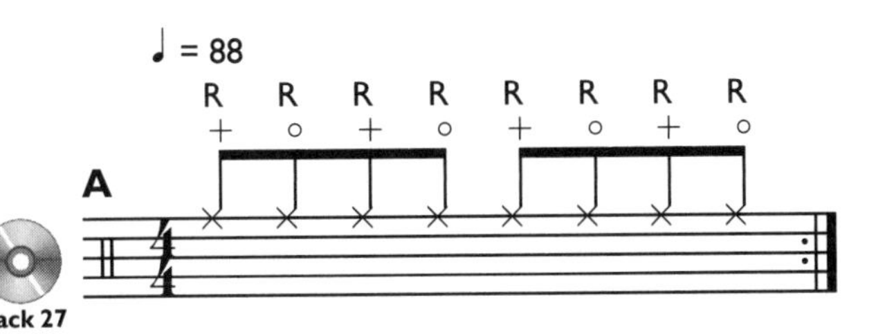

Now add the snare drum on beats 2 and 4 and the bass drum on all four beats.

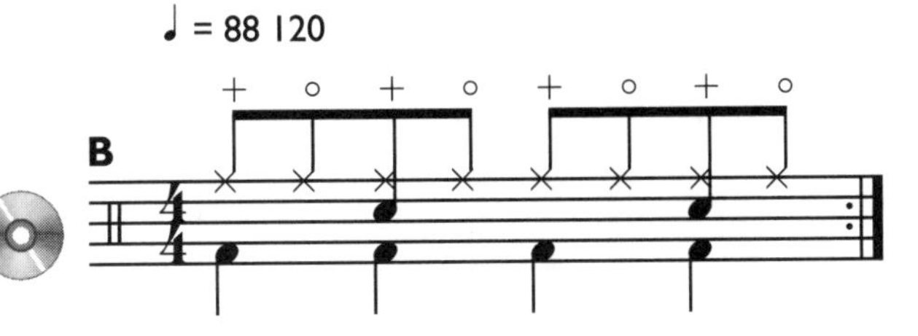

Here are some more beats using the open and closed hi-hat. This style can be heard in rock, funk and disco music.

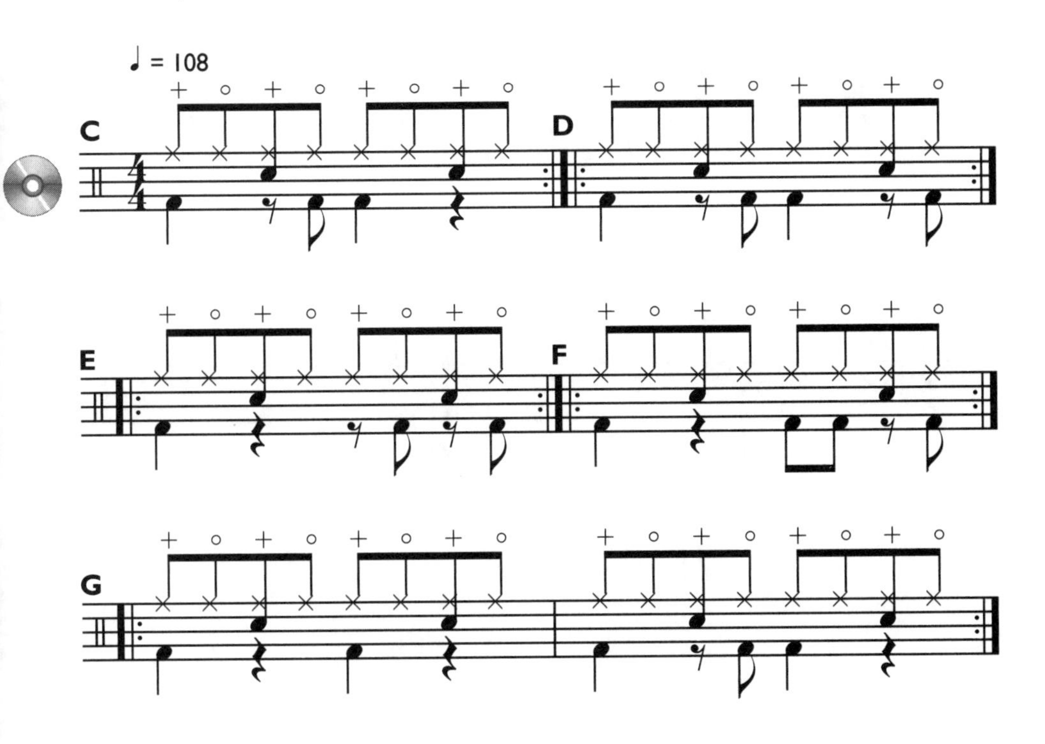

EIGHTH-NOTE SNARE-DRUM VARIATIONS

This next series of exercises will increase your ability to place a single eighth note on the snare drum anywhere within a measure. This will be a very important tool for playing more complex beats later on. To get started, we will play all four beats on the bass drum and steady eighth notes on the hi-hat. Next, we will play the snare drum with the left hand on all eight possible points within a measure. For the sake of accuracy, be sure to count as you play.

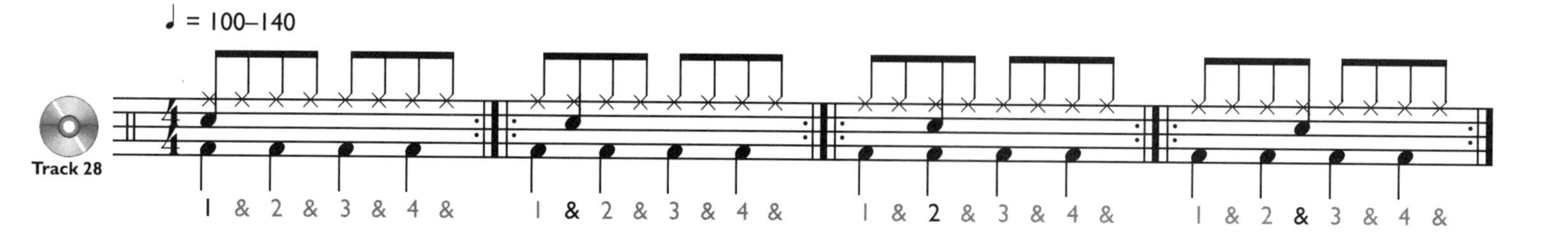

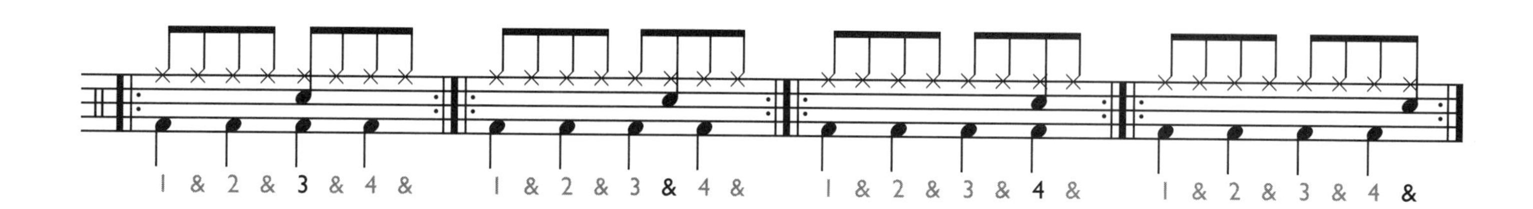

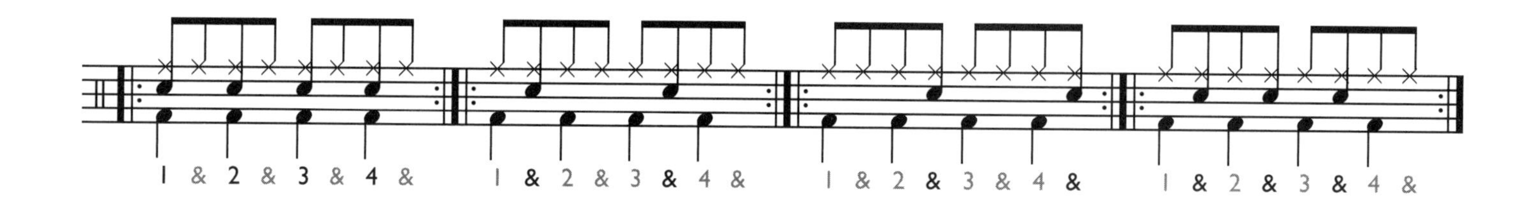

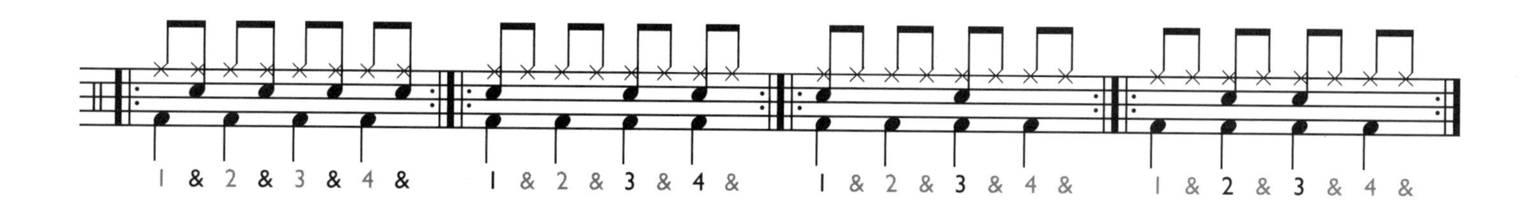

EIGHTH-NOTE SNARE-DRUM VARIATIONS (TWO NOTES)

The next step will be to play two consecutive eighth notes on the snare drum within each measure as you are playing a groove. Make sure both eighth notes on the snare are played at the same volume and are accurately placed.

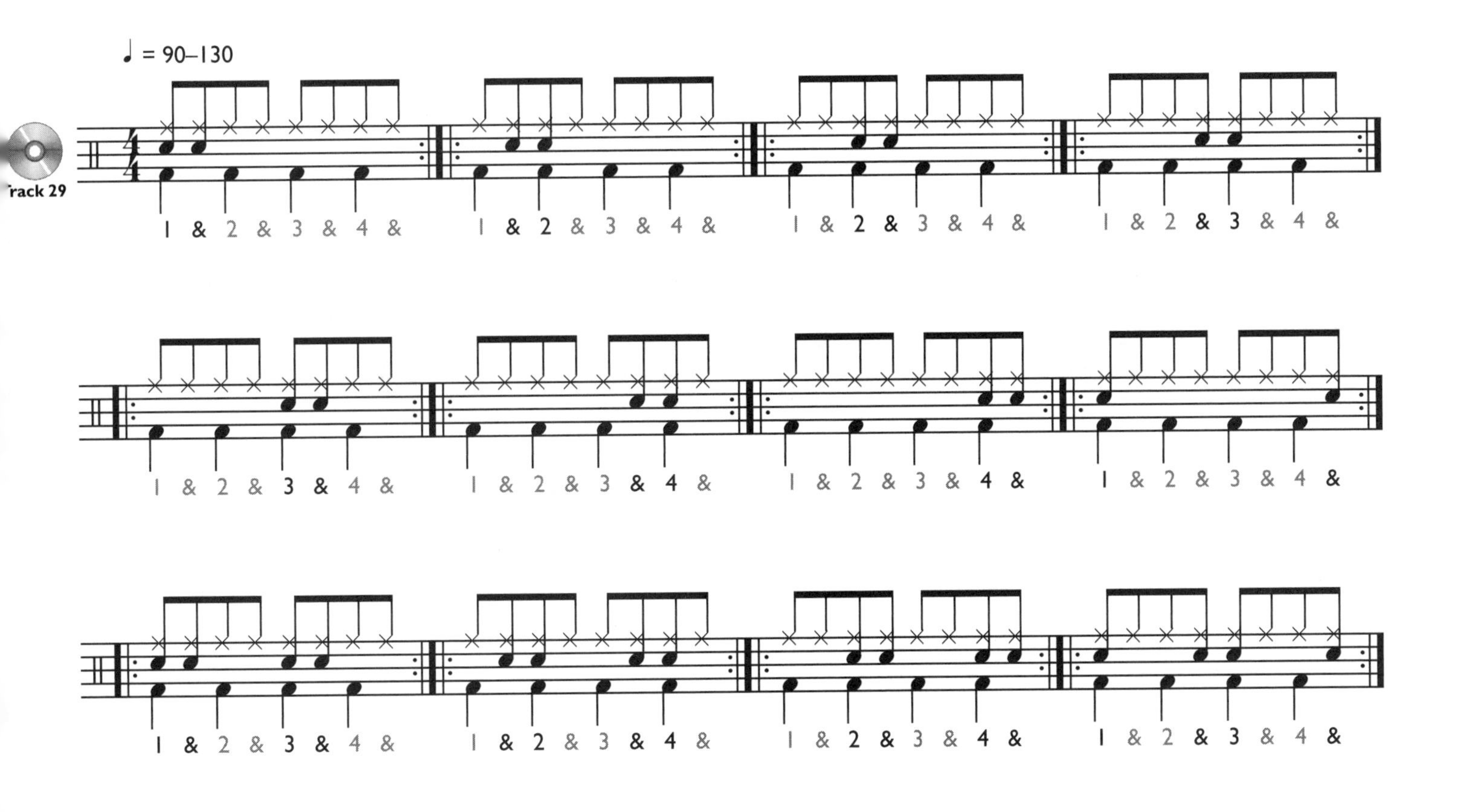

PHOTO • BOB GRUEN/COURTRSY OF STAR FILE, INC.

***Billy Cobham** (born in 1946) is generally acclaimed as fusion's greatest drummer. His explosive technique powered some of the style's most important early recordings—including groundbreaking efforts by Miles Davis and the Mahavishnu Orchestra. In these recordings,Cobham harnessed his amazing dexterity into thundering, high-octane hybrids of jazz complexity and rock aggression.*

HALF-TIME ROCK BEATS

Going into *half-time* is a very common songwriting device. This is when the basic snare drum accents on beats 2 and 4 within a rock beat are replaced with an accent on beat 3. This gives the feeling of the time "opening up;" it creates the illusion of the time being half as fast.

To get a feeling for this, let's play four measures of a regular beat followed by four measures of a half-time beat. The eighth-note pulse on the hi-hat remains the same throughout all eight measures. Only the snare hits change.

Here are a few more half-time rock beats to work on.

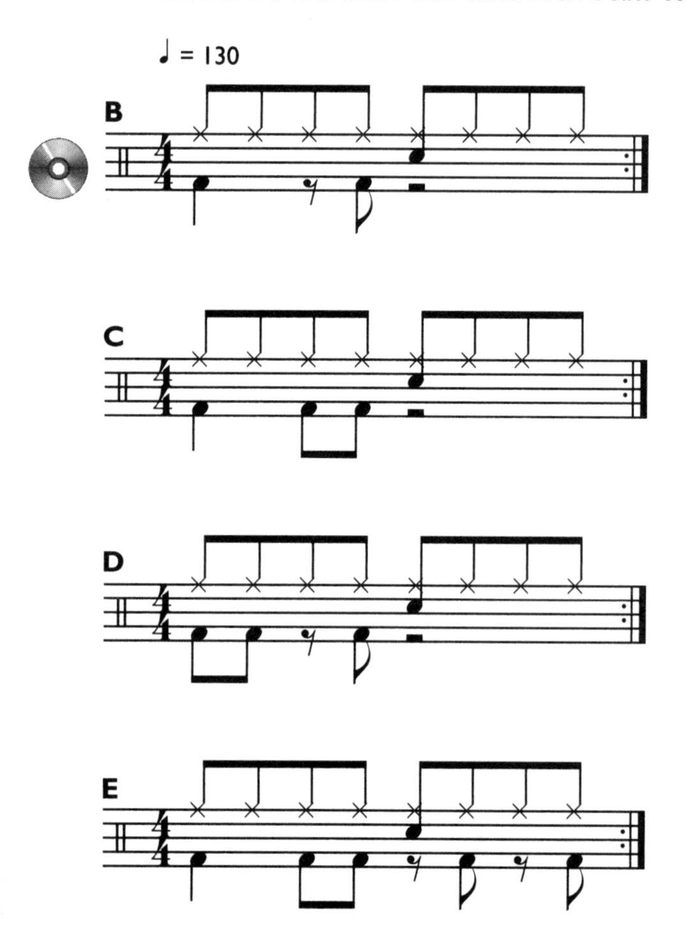

DOUBLE-TIME ROCK BEATS

Double-time is also very common in rock drumming. This is the illusion of the time speeding up or "doubling." You can hear many examples of this rhythm in heavy metal or thrash drumming.

To get this effect, play snare drum accents on all of the offbeats (all of the "&s") within the measure. Here is a double-time beat.

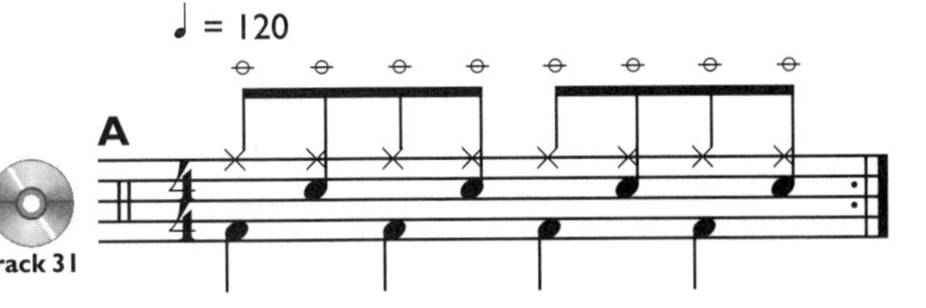

This is an example of a regular beat (the first two measures) going into a double-time beat (the last two measures).

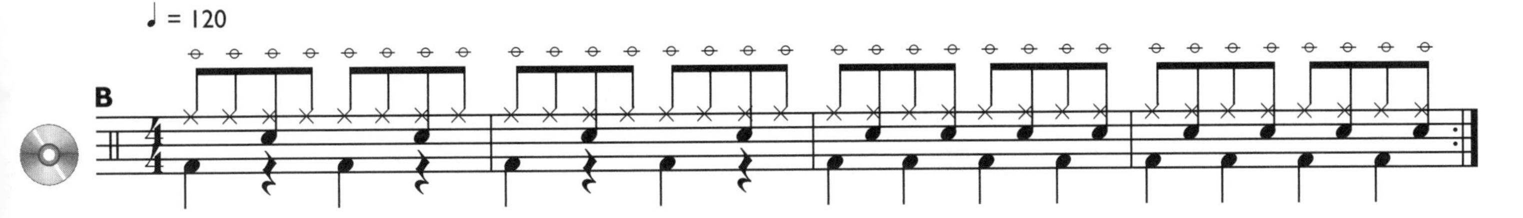

Here is another example of a double-time beat, this time accomplished by alternating snare and bass drum hits in eighth notes.

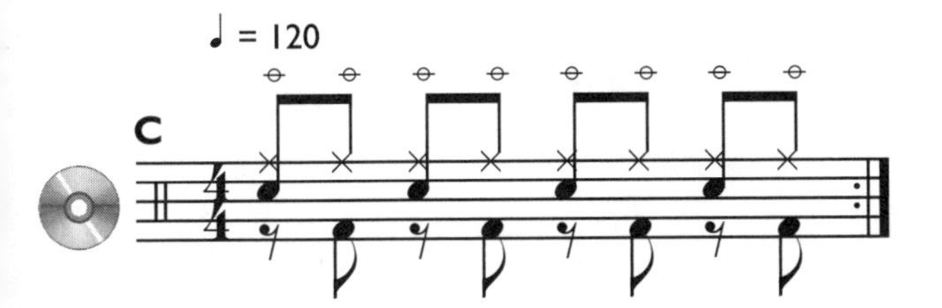

STEPPING THE HI-HAT; THE RIDE CYMBAL

Let's take those steady eighth notes we've been playing on the hi-hats and move them to the ride cymbal. If you are right-handed, the ride cymbal is usually placed on your right side (vice-versa for you lefties). When the right hand is up playing the ride, we play the hi-hat by stepping on its pedal with our left foot. This will produce a variety of different sounds and is very important in drumset playing.

To get started, play quarter notes on the hi-hat with your left foot and be sure to close the top cymbal tightly so it doesn't "splash."

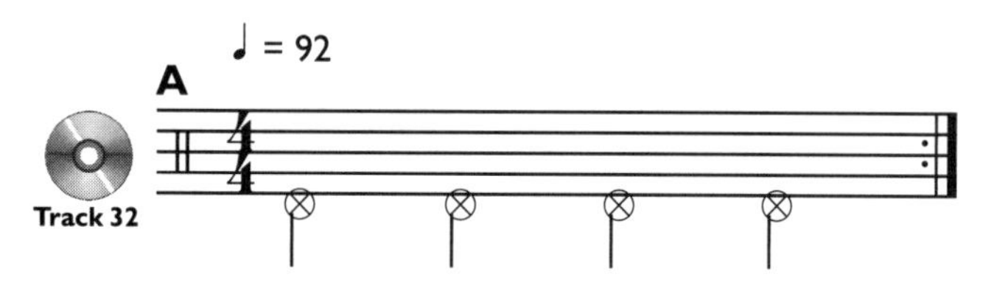

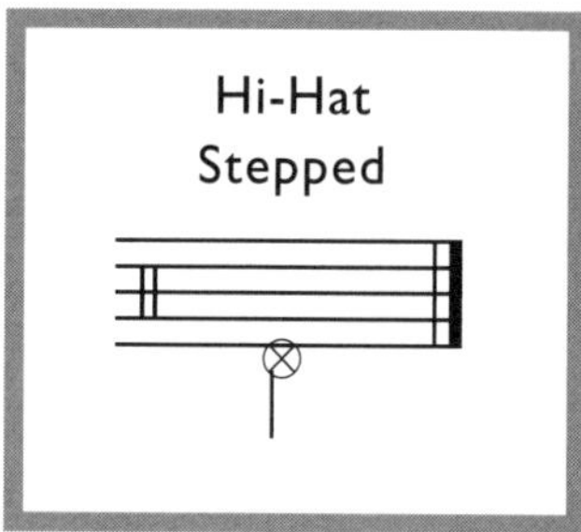

Now, play quarter notes with the right hand on the ride cymbal as you step quarters on the hi-hat with your left foot. Make sure the ride and stepped hi-hat are "locked" together (playing in exact unison).

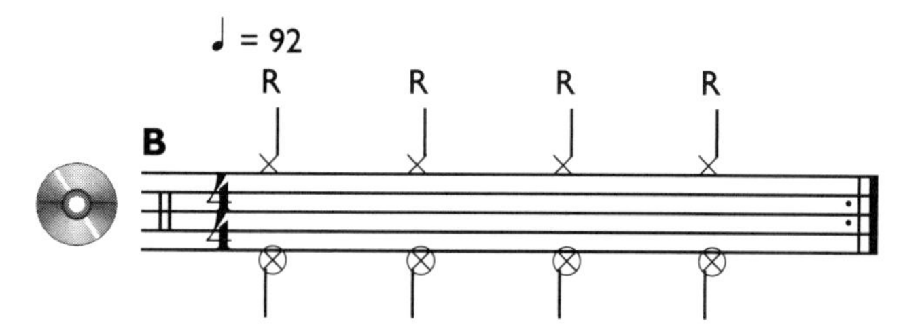

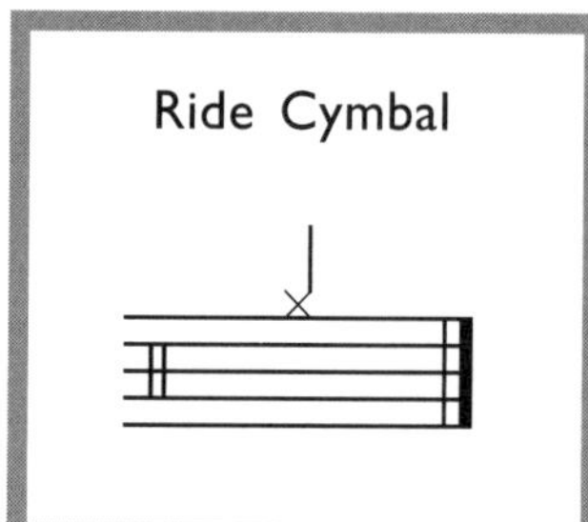

This time, play eighth notes on the ride cymbal.

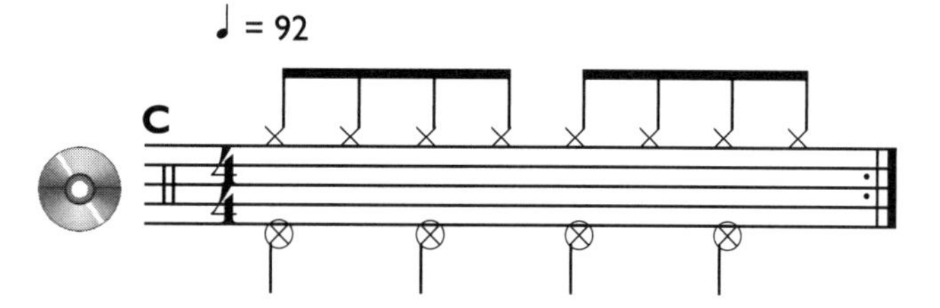

Let's add the bass drum on beats 1 and 3.

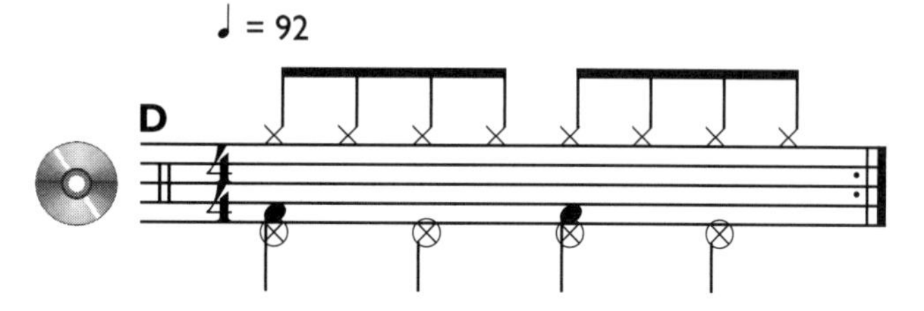

Adding the snare drum on beats 2 and 4 gives you a complete, four-way coordination beat. Take your time and work on this until it is consistent and easy.

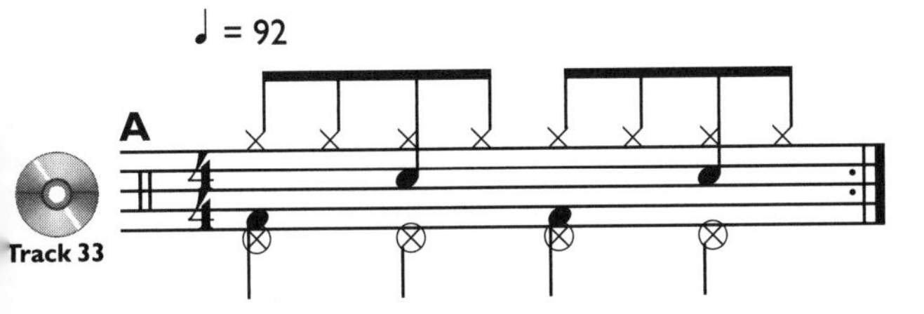

The following examples show some additional ways to use the stepped hi-hat within a rock beat.

STEPPED ON BEATS 2 AND 4

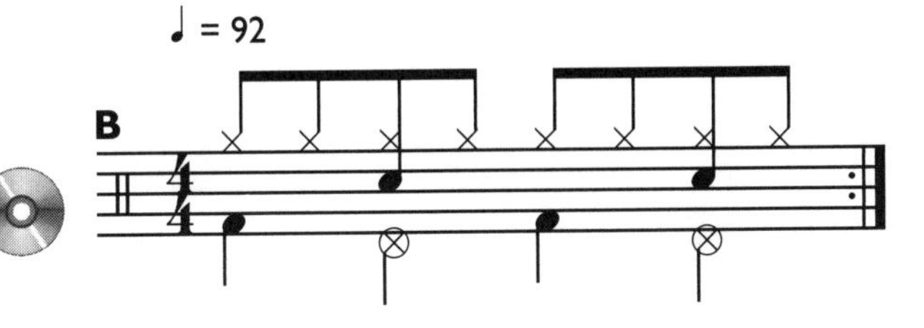

STEPPED STEADY EIGHTH NOTES WITH QUARTER NOTES ON THE RIDE

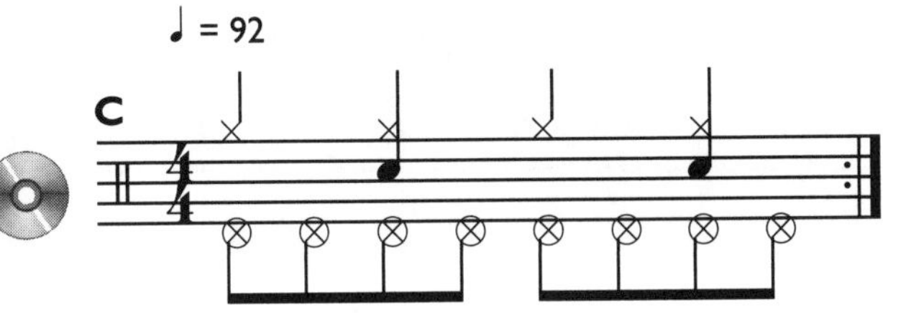

STEPPED ON ALL OF THE OFFBEATS

This is great for coordination.

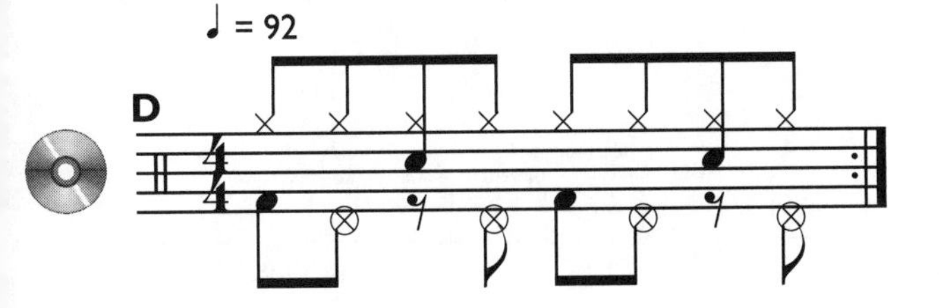

CHAPTER 5

More Eighth-Note Rock

In this chapter, we will take the beats that were covered in the last chapter and take them a few steps further. The idea will be to play one of the rock beats involving the hands and expand on it by reading eighth-note rhythms with the bass drum. This type of practice will greatly enhance your rhythmic vocabulary and expand your ability to play more difficult beats with confidence. Below are 20 groove patterns to learn. You will be combining these with bass-drum patterns from the Bass Drum Reading Source on pages 47 and 48 to create beats to practice. The highlighted measures on this page and the following pages are demonstrated on the CD that is available for this book.

20 BEAT PATTERNS

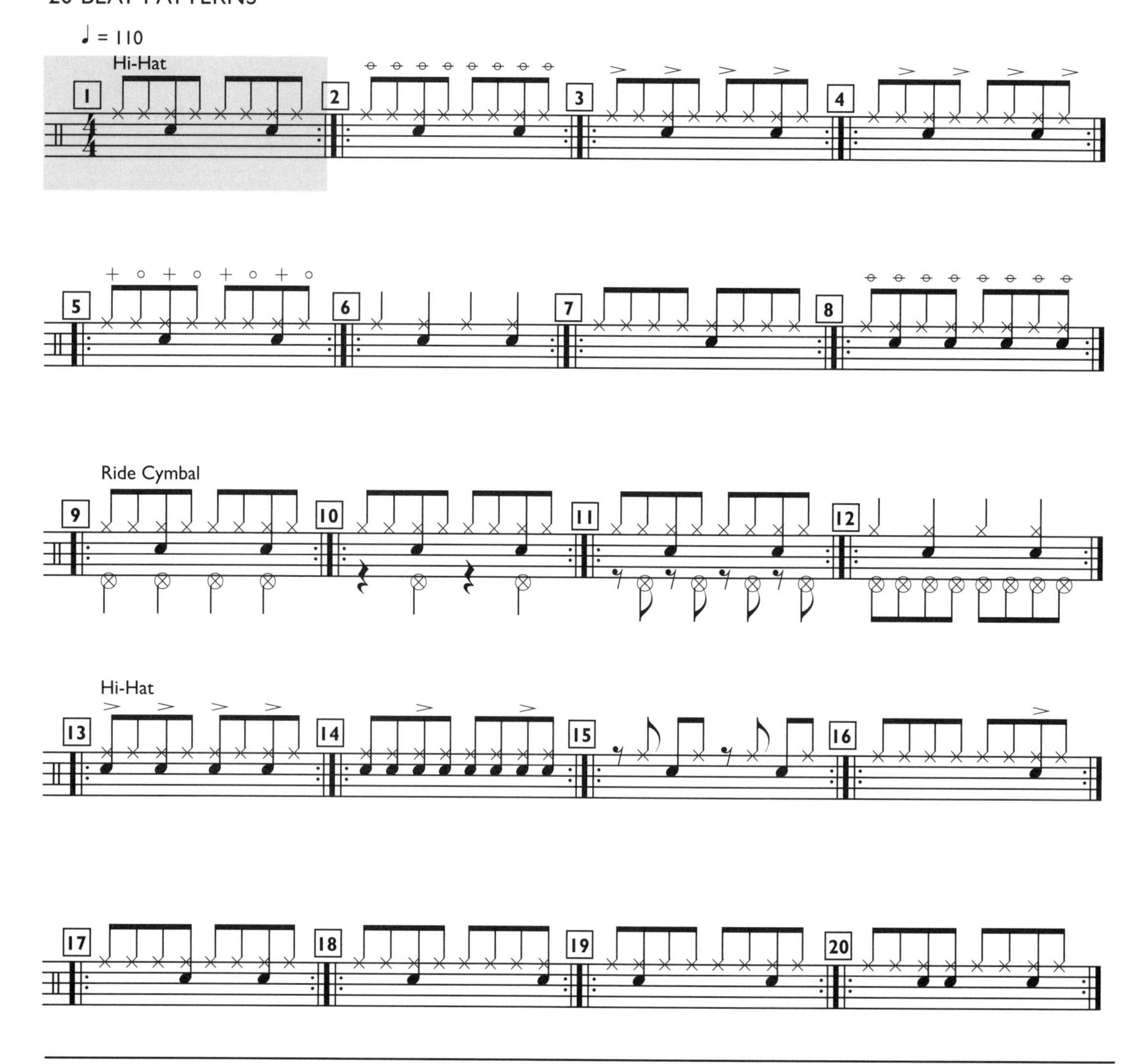

EIGHTH-NOTE READING SOURCE

Here is Part 1 of the Eighth-Note Reading Source for the bass drum rhythms. The portions that are performed on the CD that is available with this book are highlighted: Beat Pattern No. 1 over the first four bars of Part 1 and Part 2 of the Reading Source.

Part 1

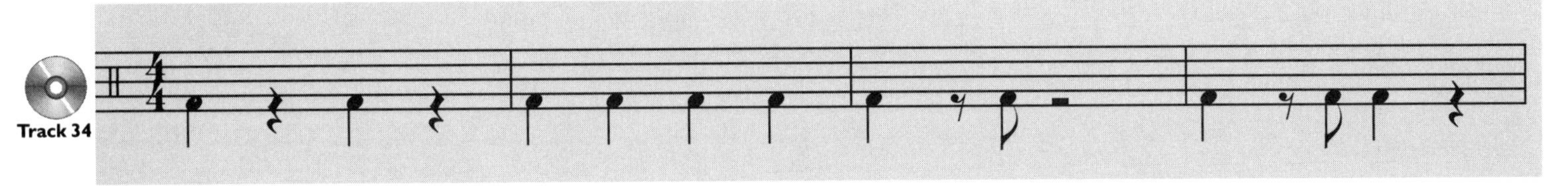

EIGHTH-NOTE READING SOURCE

PRACTICE PROCEDURE

Take some time and read through the Eighth-Note Reading Source on pages 47 and 48 so that you fully understand each rhythm and can play each one accurately. The next step will be to use the Reading Source as the bass drum line while playing one of the 20 Beat Patterns from page 46. Let's take Beat No. 1 from Part 1 and play the first measure of the Reading Source on the bass drum.

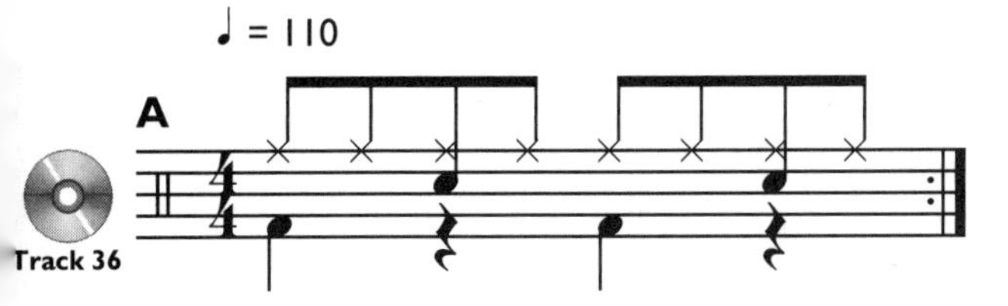

Now let's play the first two measures from Part 1 of the Reading Source on the bass drum.

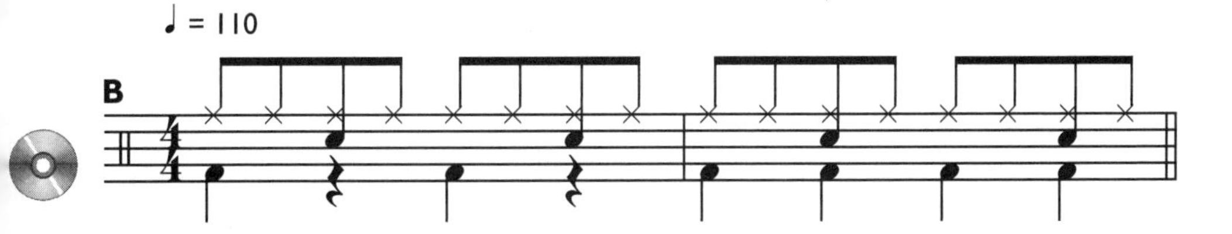

Try using the first four measures from Part 1 of the Reading Source.

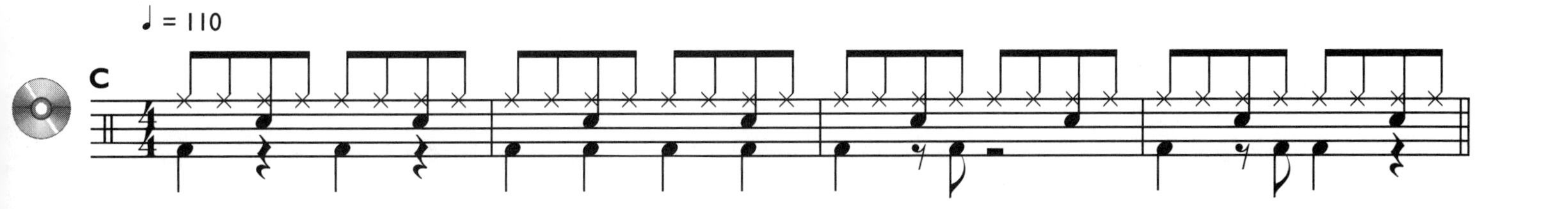

Here are the first four measures from Part 1 of the Reading Source applied to Beat No. 5 from page 46.

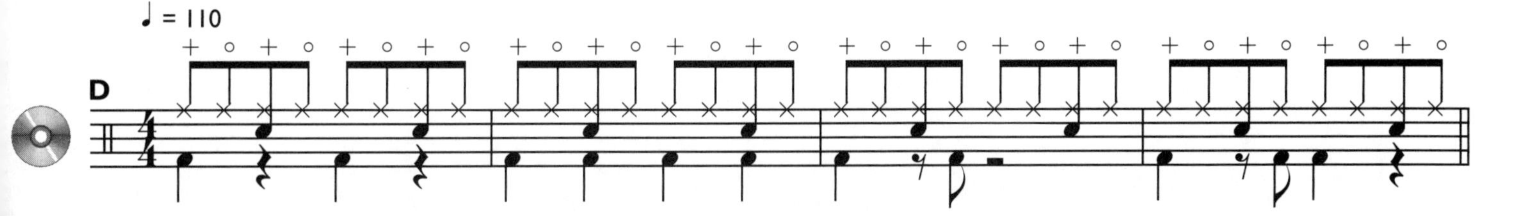

PRACTICE CONSIDERATIONS FOR THE 20 BEAT PATTERNS AND BASS-DRUM READING SOURCE

When practicing the 20 Beat Patterns in combination withthe Bass-Drum Reading Source, go slowly at first and take one beat pattern and one measure of reading source at a time. Move on only when you can play each bass-drum variation well every time. It's not a race to the bottom of the page! This kind of practice will yield great results when you are patient and consistent.

The goal is to be able to play any beat pattern with any bass drum variation. There isn't a quick way to reach that goal; only a thorough process such as this will work. Here are a few suggestions for practicing this section.

1. **Practice with a metronome.** It is preferable to use a metronome with headphones when practicing at the drumset. This is essential for maintaining your focus. If a particular idea is giving you trouble, slow down the tempo until you can play it consistently. The metronome will help you keep good time, and you will need to *practice* good time in order to *perform* good time with other people.

2. **Play the ideas for four and eight measures before moving on.** This way the groove will have time to feel more natural to you. You must spend some time with repetition.

3. **Record yourself practicing.** By listening back to yourself, you can get a great idea of how you sound and what needs improvement. Make the necessary adjustments to get things to lock in and groove.

4. **Make your practice fun!** Practicing your instrument should be enjoyable, not grim duty. Look for ways to make practicing fun and you will spend more time doing it.

   One suggestion is to take these eighth-note groove exercises and work on them while playing along with a recording of some of your favorite music. You can use the tempo of the songs as your tempo for the exercises.

   Another suggestion is to get together with other musicians and practice. Also, you can get together with a fellow drummer and work on different beats.

CHAPTER 6

Introducing Sixteenth Notes

After working extensively with eighth notes, it's time to move on to *sixteenth notes*. Sixteenth notes are twice as fast as eighth notes, and can be easily identified by the *double flag* on the stem. *Double beams* connect consecutive sixteenth notes.

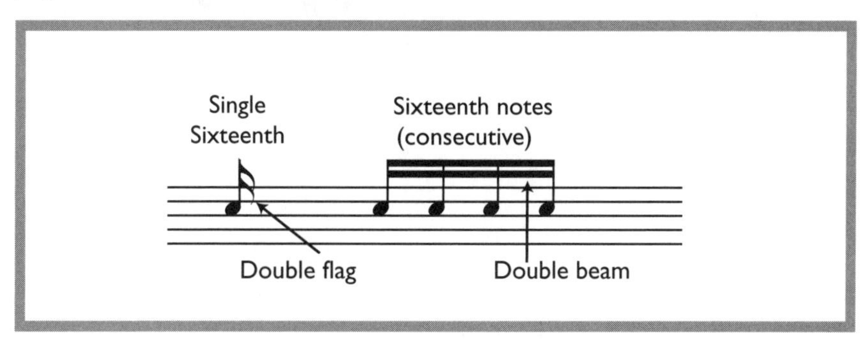

Sixteenth notes are counted like this: 1–e–&–a, 2–e–&–a, 3–e–&–a, 4–e–&–a.

An easy way to make the transition from eighth notes to sixteenth notes is to first play eighth notes with the right hand.

Now divide each eighth note into two parts by adding notes in between the eighth notes with the left hand while still playing eighths with the right hand. Voila! Sixteenth notes.

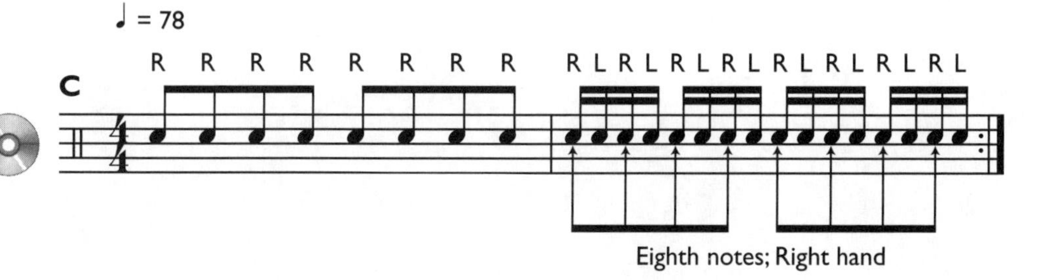

SIXTEENTH-NOTE TRANSITION EXERCISES

Here's an exercise to help you become more comfortable with the transition from quarter notes to eighth notes to sixteenth notes. Use a metronome and strive for accuracy. When you move to each new note value you are essentially doubling the time, so make sure you are subdividing the time correctly.

Another way to lock up with the sixteenth note value is to play accents. In this exercise, accent each quarter note with the right hand as you play a single-stroke roll.

It is also helpful to accent all of the right-hand strokes, giving you an emphasis on the eighth notes as you are playing sixteenth notes.

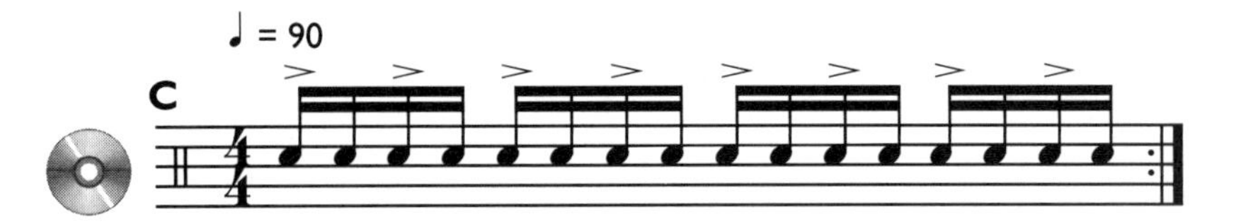

Be sure to count the exercises in this chapter first. You must be able to *count* even sixteenth notes before you *play* sixteenth notes.

SIXTEENTH-NOTE READING EXERCISES

The following set of exercises will help you become more familiar with reading sixteenth notes. The first exercise is sixteenth notes grouped in sets of fours. It is essential that you count and use a metronome as you practice this material. Each sixteenth note must be accurately placed.

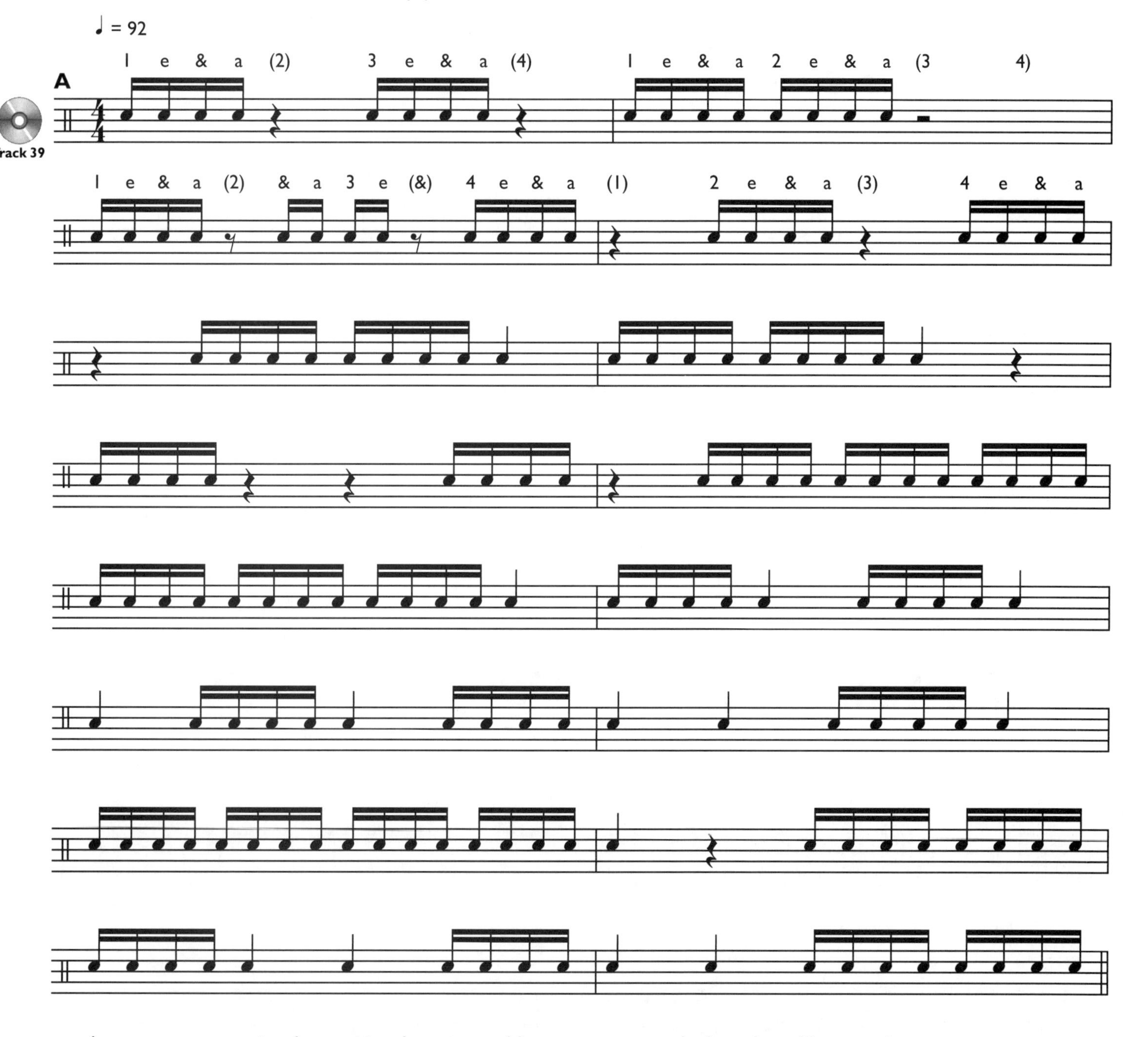

A great way to practice the exercise above is to add quarter notes on the bass drum. Here are the first four measures with quarter notes on the bass drum. Apply this idea to the entire exercise.

SIXTEENTH-NOTE READING EXERCISES WITH RESTS

The following reading exercises will incorporate the *sixteenth rest.* Be sure to count as you are playing these examples and give each rest its full value.

The sixteenth rest: 

SIXTEENTH NOTE READING WITH GROUPS OF THREE NOTES

Sixteenth notes can be combined with eighth notes to create groups of three notes played in the space of one beat. The single beat of the eighth note is connected to the double beam of the sixteenth notes.

These combinations are very common in various styles of music. Let's take a look at each one individually before we practice them in a reading exercise.

In this reading exercise, play quarter notes on the bass drum throughout. Remember that the tempo marking indicated is only a suggestion, and you can play any exercise faster or slower according to your comfort level.

SIXTEENTH-NOTE ACCENT STUDIES

SINGLE ACCENT

In this next series of exercises, we will play a single-stroke roll as sixteenth notes and work on adding accents. This will give you total control over placing a sixteenth note in any part of the beat.

To get started, let's work on a single accent in each beat. Play quarter notes on the bass drum and concentrate on making the accents strong and the unaccented notes very quiet. Notice how the bass drum hits will clarify where the quarter note is in relation to the accented sixteenth notes.

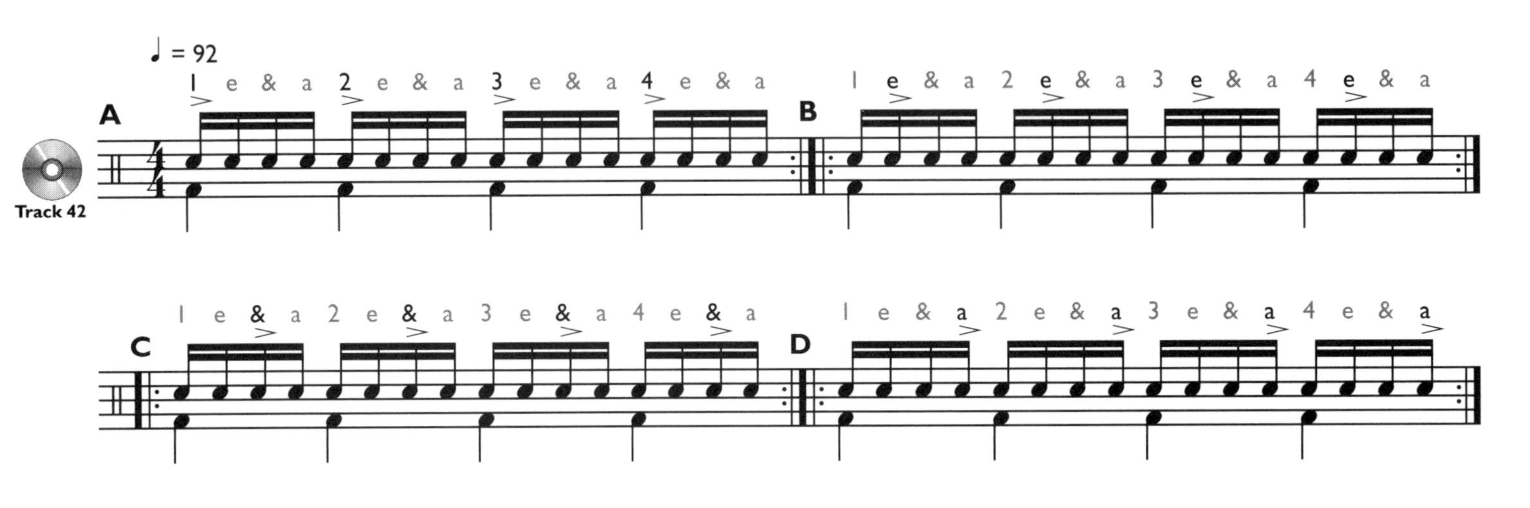

This exercise has one measure of a non-accented roll and one measure of an accented roll.

PHOTO • JIM FURMANOVSKY/COURTESY OF STAR FILE PHOTO, INC.

***John Bonham** was the drummer for Led Zeppelin from the group's founding in 1968 until his death in 1980. His innovative recordings with Led Zeppelin continue to influence drummers today.*

TWO ACCENTS

The next step will be to work on two accented sixteenth notes while playing the single stroke roll. Again, play quarter notes the bass drum as you are practicing these exercises. Make sure you count as you are doing this.

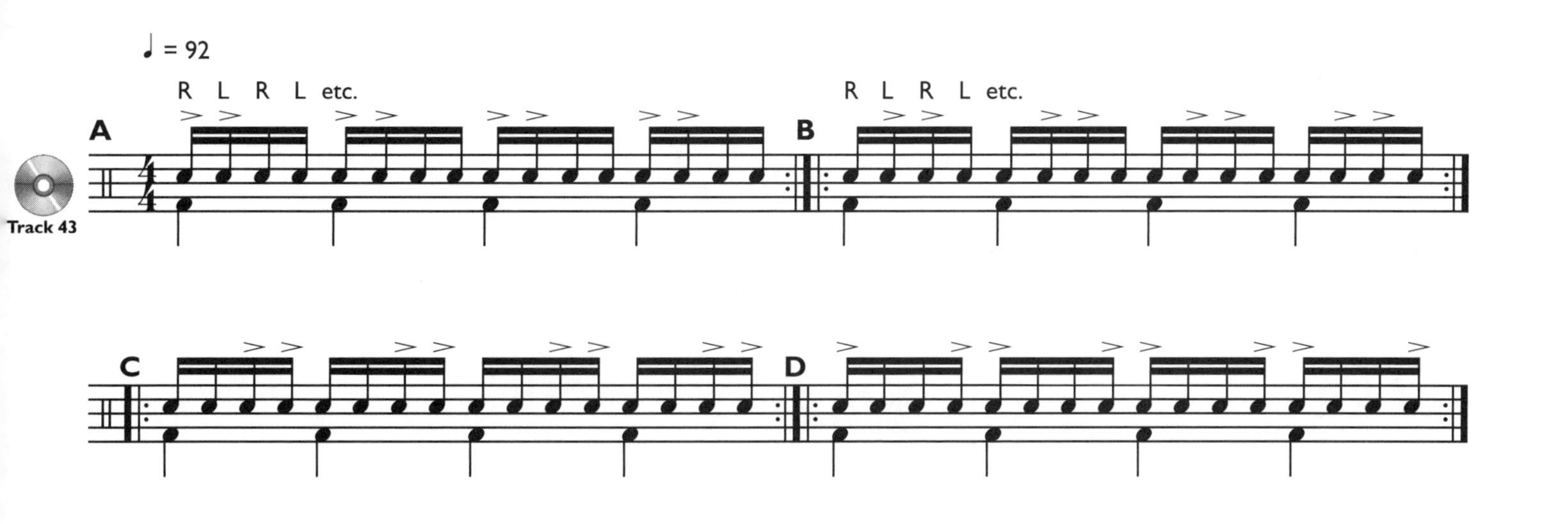

APPLYING ACCENTS TO THE DRUMSET

Let's take the accents we've been practicing and use them on different instruments of the drumset. We will start by playing the accented notes on the tom tom and the unaccented notes on the snare drum. Play quarter notes on the bass drum and step the hi-hat on beats 2 and 4.

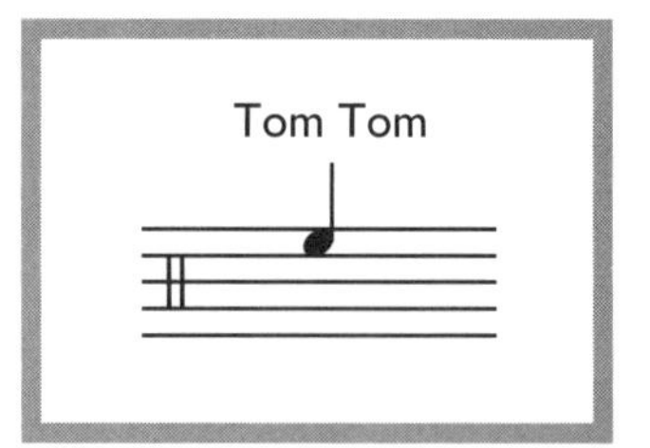

Now we'll split up the accented roll a little further and use both the floor tom and tom-tom. All right-handed accents will be played on the floor tom, all left-handed accents on the tom-tom and all unaccented strokes on the snare drum. This exercise should give you an indication of the various possibilities of the drumset.

CHAPTER 7

Getting Around the Drumset

In this chapter, we will work on ways to gain facility getting around the drumset. The drumset is a collection of instruments that contains not only drums, but cymbals as well. In order to incorporate all of these elements into our playing, we have to be familiar with the territory. The following series of exercises will help you to do just that. You will gain speed, accuracy and endurance while playing on the complete set.

BASS DRUM AND SNARE DRUM WORKOUT

These exercises are designed to increase your sense of interplay between the hands and feet. You should practice these examples with both the heel-up and flat-footed techniques on the bass drum pedal to develop both ways of playing. This first example is a single-stroke roll between the snare and bass drum.

SINGE-STROKE EXERCISE

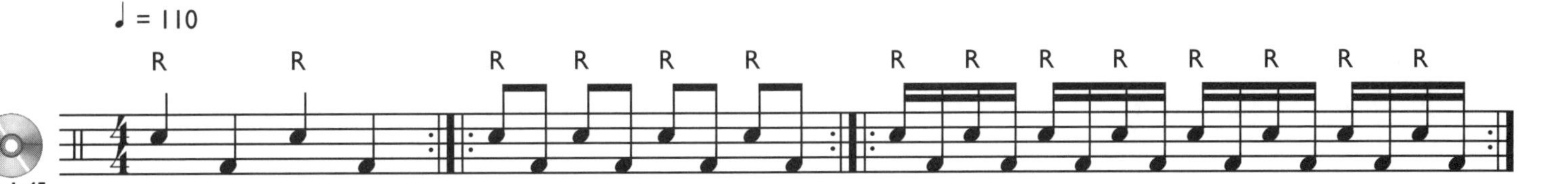

Alternative Stickings:
R–L–R–L
or all Lefts

PHOTO • JOE SIA/COURTESY OF STAR FILE PHOTO, INC.

__Neil Peart__ is the drummer and lyricist for the Canadian rock trio Rush, an immensely popular group since the mid-1970s. His flawless technique and fluency in playing in unusual time signatures are two of the elements that give the group its characteristic sound.

DOUBLE-STROKE EXERCISE

The next series of exercises will have two notes on the snare followed by two on the bass drum. These, like the previous exercises, are essential and frequently-used movements. These exercises isolate them for the sake of practice. When the basic idea is up to speed, it is much easier to apply the concept in an actual musical context. Make sure that both strokes on the snare and bass drum are even sounding at a slow-to-moderate tempo before speeding up.

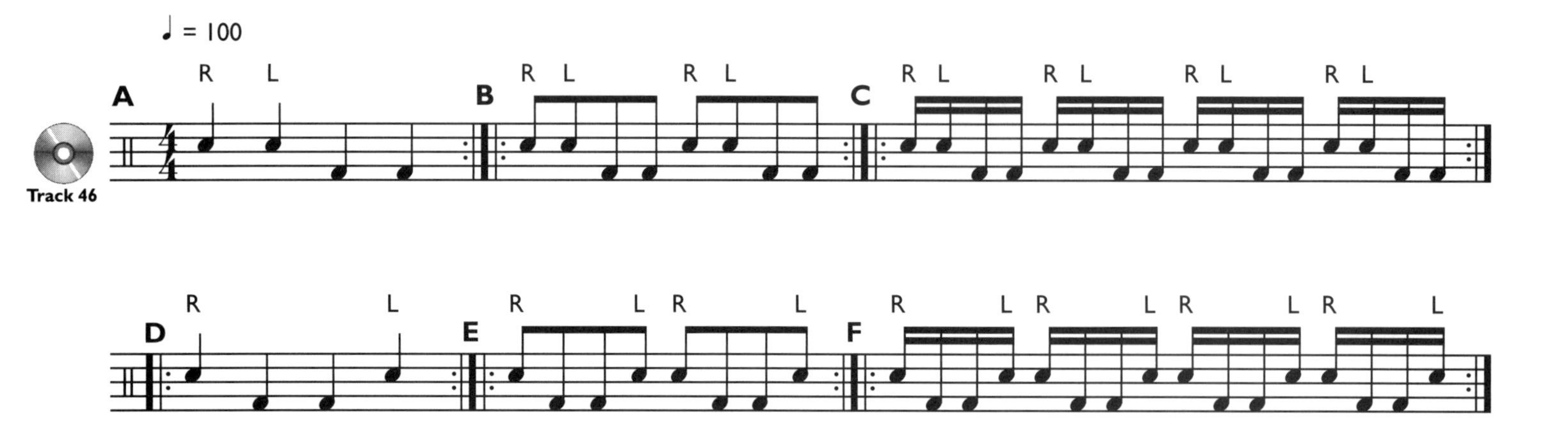

COMBINATION EXERCISE

This exercise is a combination of single- and double-strokes for the snare and bass drum.

MOVING AROUND THE SET WITH SINGLE STROKES

Here are some exercises to get you moving around the drumset while playing a single-stroke roll. The two basic movements around the set use clockwise and counter-clockwise motion. In order to get comfortable and familiar with these moves, you will need to practice slowly and accurately.

Keep these things in mind when playing:

- Hit the center of each drum.
- Avoid hitting the rims or hitting the sticks together and strive for a good, clean sound.
- Keep your eyes focused on the instrument.
- Make your arm movement fluid and natural.
- Don't tighten up your grip as you play.

These exercises should be practiced with quarter notes on the bass drum and hi-hat hits on beats 2 and 4.

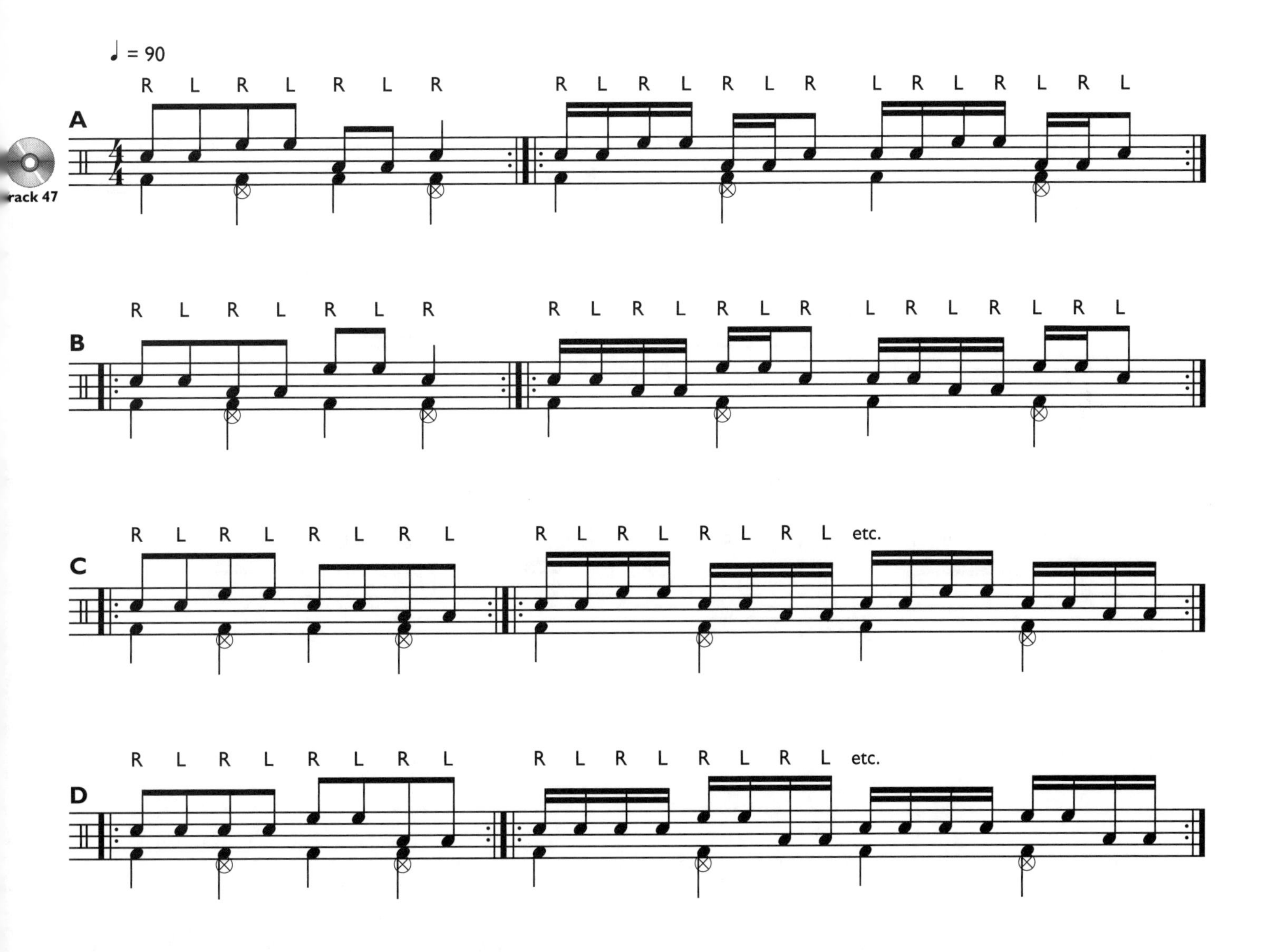

The next series of exercises will explore some useful movements around the set. Learn the patterns slowly before playing them fast. If necessary, you can start slower than the suggested tempo. When you're ready, try going faster.

MOVING AROUND THE SET WITH DOUBLE STROKES

Now let's apply the double-stroke roll around the set. The indicated sticking, when mastered, will allow you to play some intricate things on the set. If you have any difficulty performing any of these movements, spend some time practicing the double-stroke roll on the snare drum or drum pad for a while before applying it to the set.

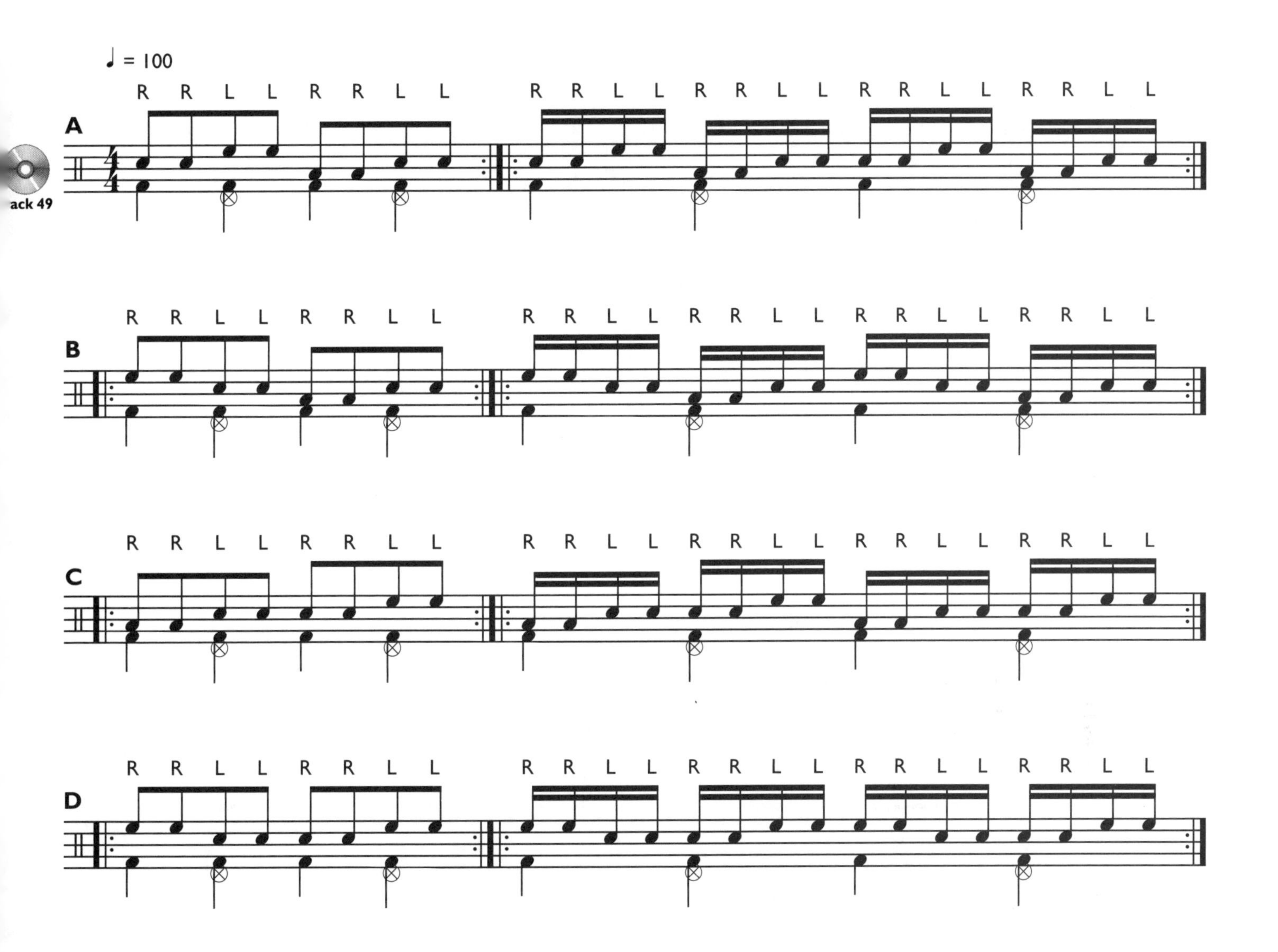

HAND AND FOOT COMBINATIONS AROUND THE SET

Now let's take some of those hand and foot combinations you've learned and apply them to the full drumset. Good stickings are essential for ease of movement at the set and a good knowledge of various stickings gives you more options. Remember the stickings indicated for each exercise are only there to get you started. You are encouraged to expand on the sticking patterns and come up with some of your own.

THE CRASH CYMBALS AND SINGLE-STROKES

In this series of exercises you will be using the right and left crash cymbals on the drumset. If you only have one crash cymbal, consider adding a second, but go ahead and do all of the exercises with just one for now. To get started, let's begin with an exercise to get us familiar with hitting a crash cymbal and bass drum at the same time. Count throughout the exercise to insure accuracy.

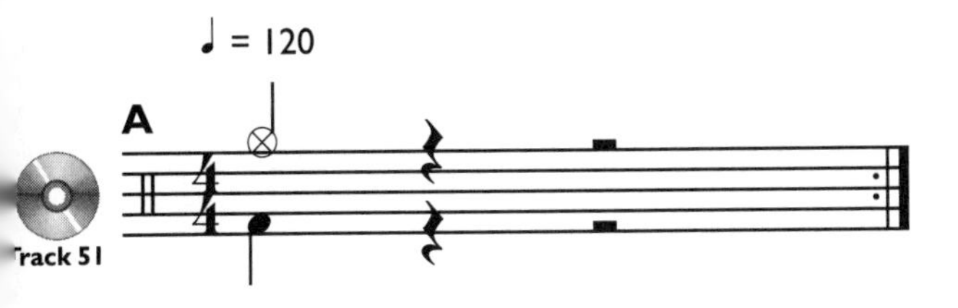

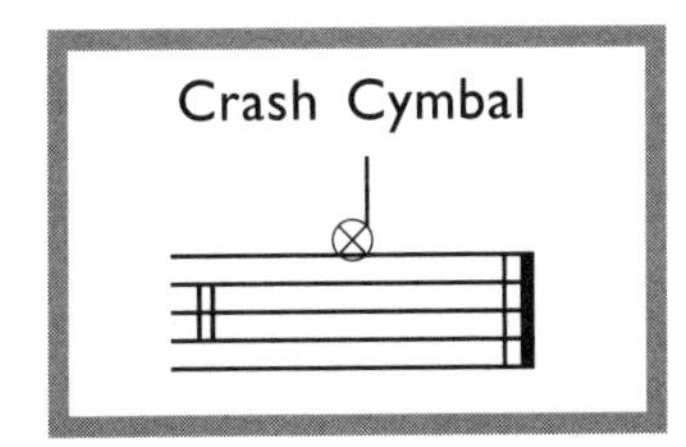

Now play a single-stroke roll on the snare drum with an accent on beat 1. Play the bass drum together with the accent on beat 1.

Move the accented note on beat 1 to the crash cymbal (if you have two, the one on your right side) while continuing the roll on the snare drum. Double the crash note with the bass drum to give it some extra punch!

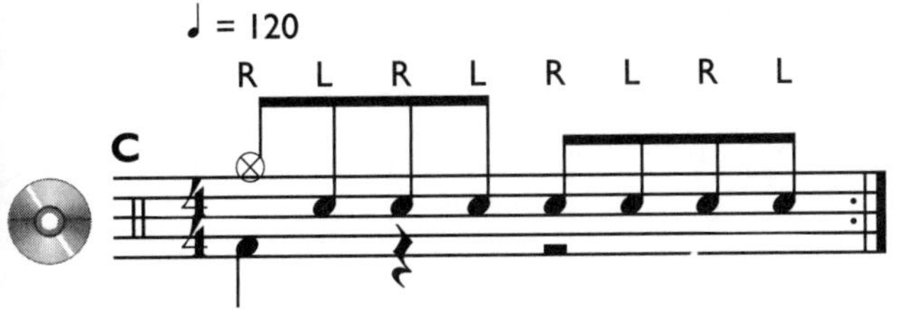

CRASH CYMBAL EXERCISES

When the exercises on page 65 feel comfortable, move on to these variations of the basic idea. The crashed notes with the bass drum should sound "tight." The trick is to hit both simultaneously. Make sure that the snare drum roll is very smooth sounding. This will mean getting the hand that has just hit the crash cymbal back to the snare drum to continue the roll. These exercises will help prepare you to play drum fills and solos. Take your time and make everything flow.

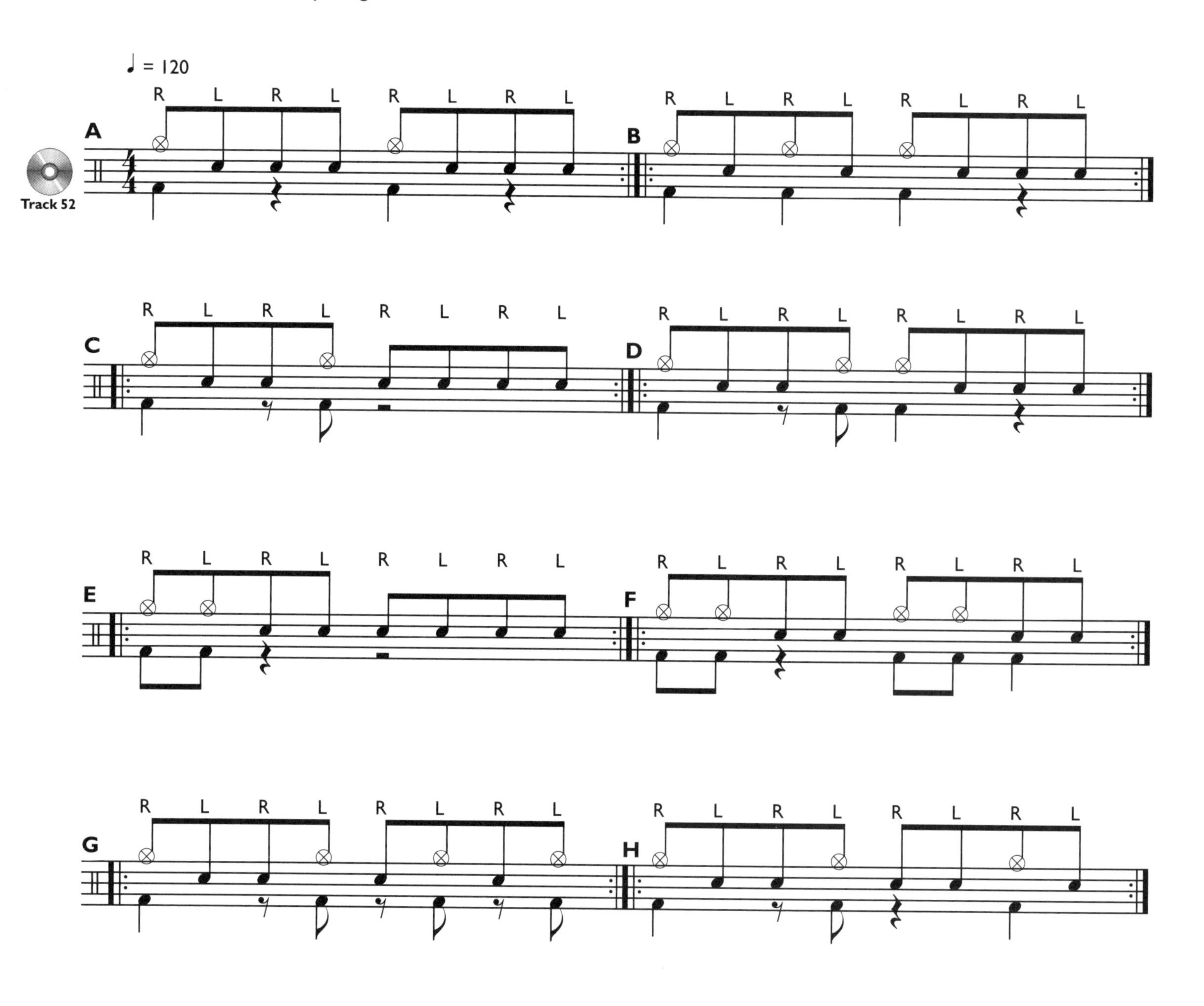

APPLYING THE EXERCISES TO DRUM BEATS

The next step is to take some of the drumset exercises you've been working on and apply them in a musical way to drum beats. First, let's look at several two-measure beats. The idea is to play two measures of a beat followed by two measures of a single-stroke roll around the set.

Play this two-measure beat.

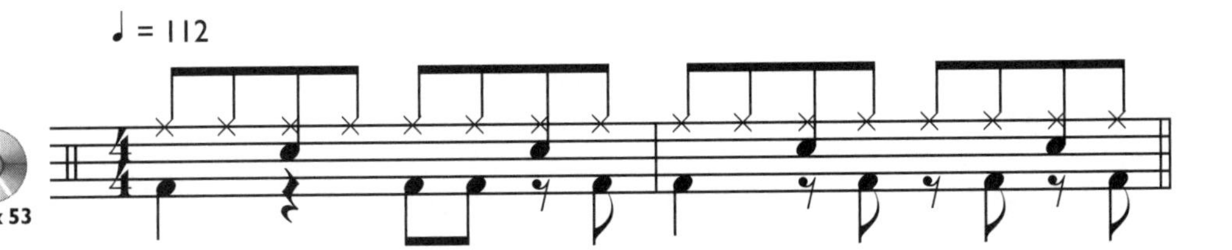

Then play one of the following two-measure moves around the set. It is a good idea to learn the move around the set well before adding it to the drum beat.

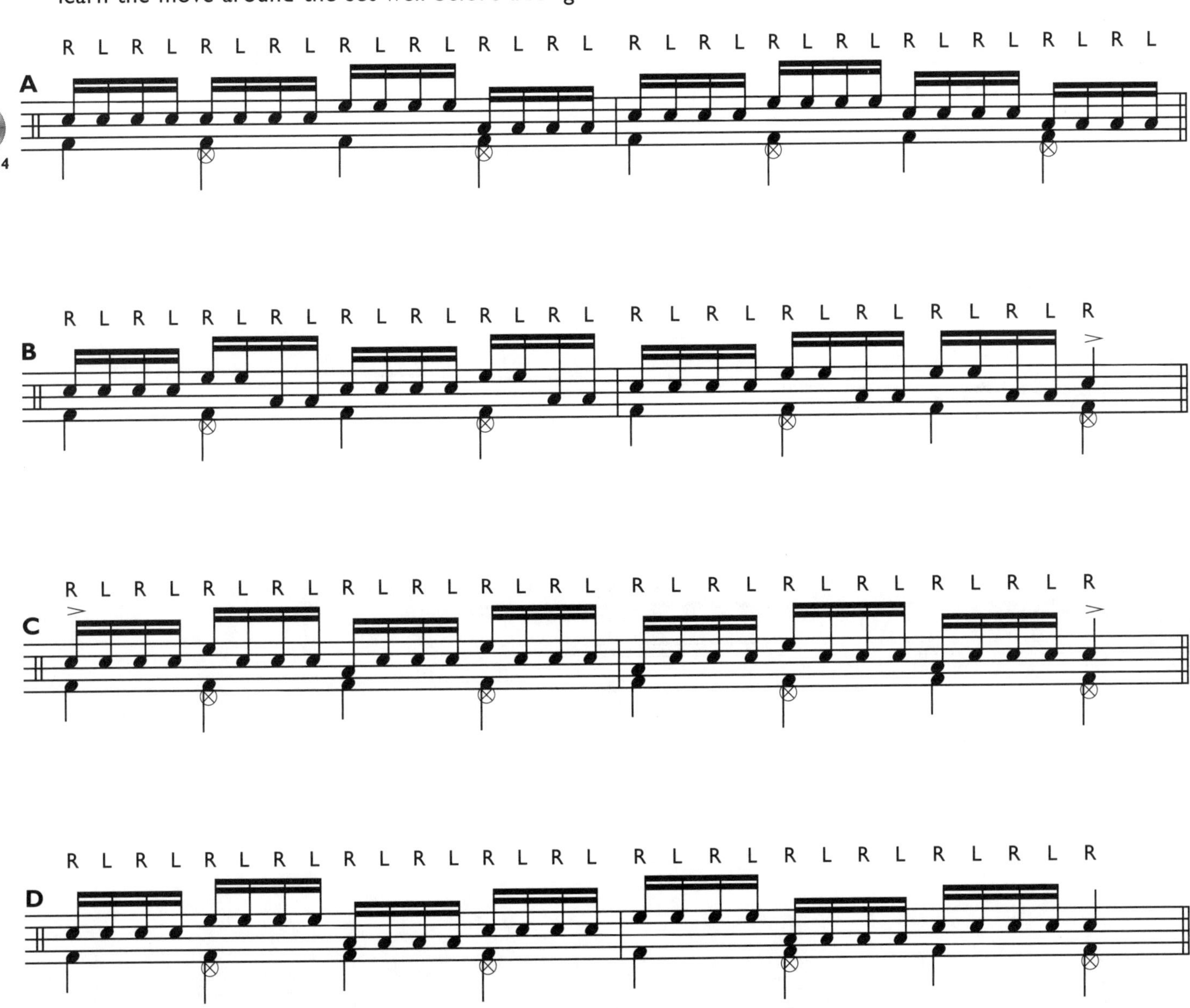

CHAPTER 8

Sixteenth-Note Beats

In this chapter, you will make the transition from eighth-note oriented beats to playing grooves that involve sixteenth notes. Do not rush this transition. Before you continue in this chapter, you should be extremely proficient with eighth-note beats.

Now, instead of eight different choices for where to play in a measure, you have sixteen. You must be very accurate. Good counting skills are crucial to accurately perform these beats. This is non-negotiable! Every great drummer has had to go through this process and master this ability.

To get started, work on this counting exercise. As discussed in Chapter 6, you must be able to *count* even sixteenth notes before you *play* sixteenth notes. This will help you internalize the sixteenth-note pulse.

Play sixteenth notes on your hi-hat as a single stroke roll. Play the bass drum on all four beats. Count aloud as you play.

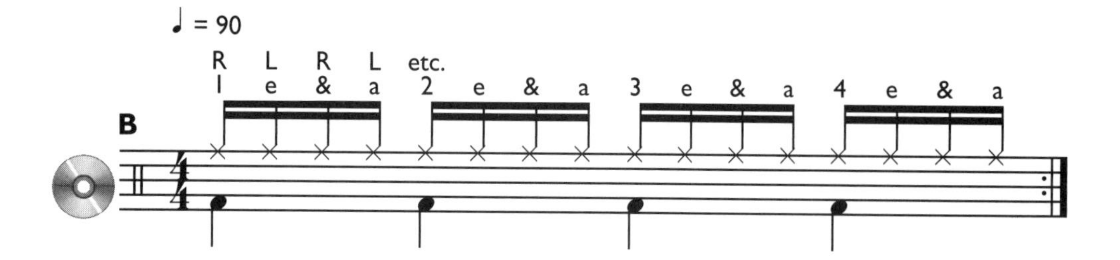

SIXTEENTH-NOTE HI-HAT BEATS

Play sixteenth notes on the hi-hat using the single-stroke roll. Play beats 2 and 4 on the snare drum with your right hand. Keep the sixteenth-note pulse on the hi-hat flowing evenly.

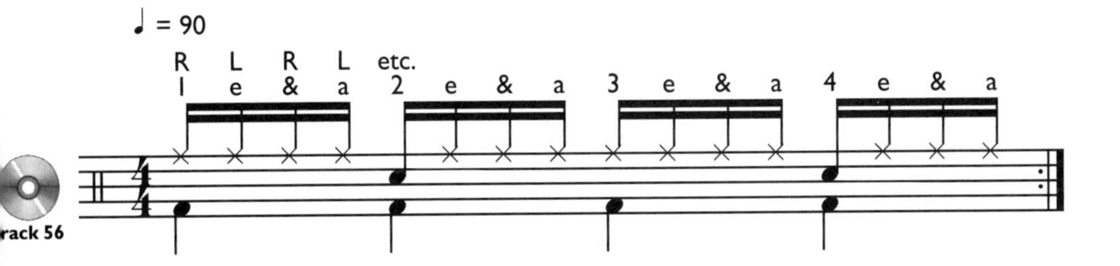

Track 56

Here's the same beat with a few variations on the bass drum.

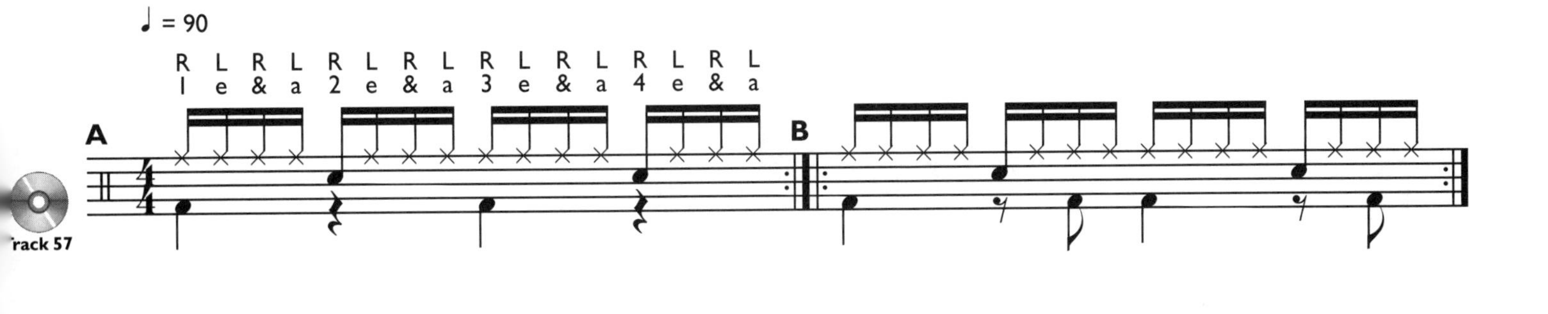

Track 57

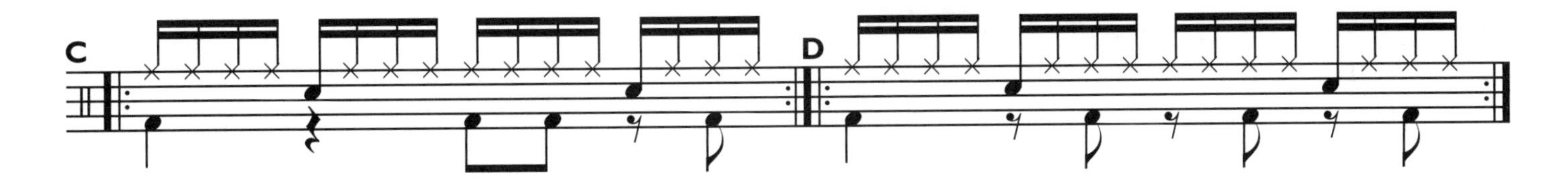

ONE-HANDED SIXTEENTH-NOTE HI-HAT BEATS

The following series of beats are built on a continuous flow of sixteenth notes played on the hi-hat by the right hand. This is great for your right-hand endurance. Play these beats slowly at first and try not to tighten up your grip as you are playing. If you feel fatigued or your arms feel tight, stop playing and spend more time playing at a slightly slower tempo.

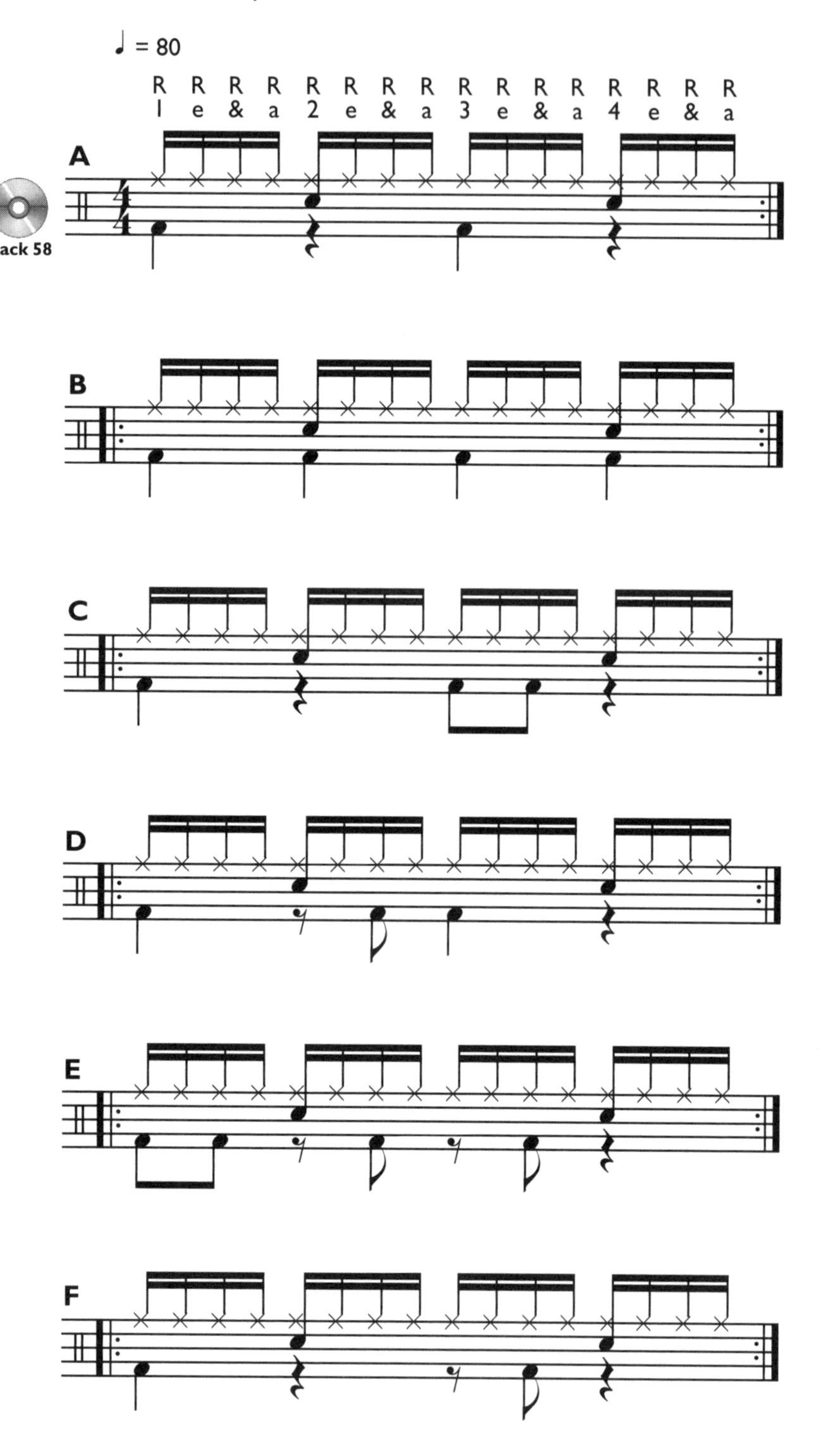

ADDING SIXTEENTH NOTES TO THE SNARE DRUM

Let's add a few sixteenth notes to the basic groove we have been working on. These variations will be played on the snare drum with the left hand as you are playing constant sixteenth notes on the hi-hat with the right hand. Notice how the offbeats played on the snare drum are in unison with the hi-hat part. This will help you lock into the sixteenth-note feel.

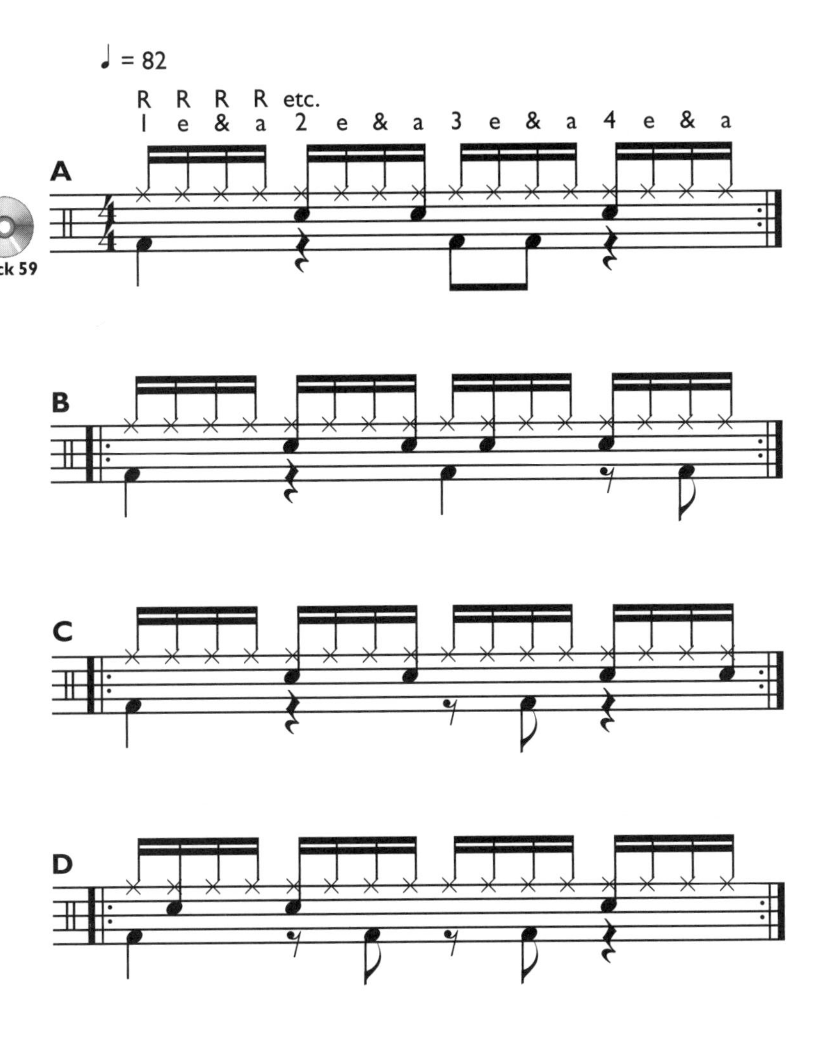

Here's an example of playing an accent on the first part of every beat in the hi-hat part. This will reinforce the quarter note as you are playing sixteenths.

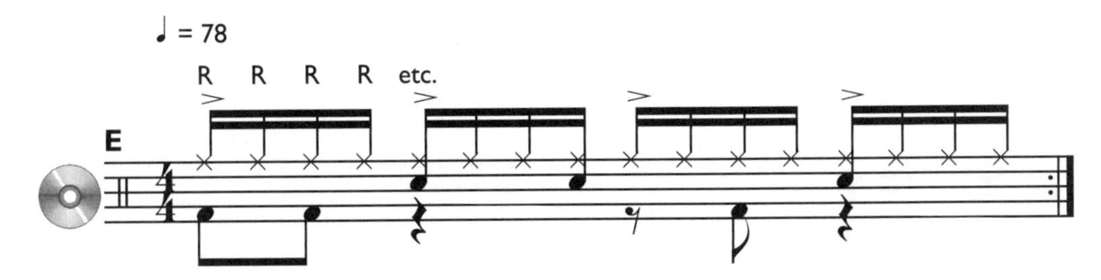

ADDING SIXTEENTH NOTES TO THE BASS DRUM

Let's take some of those offbeat sixteenth notes and play them on the bass drum. Again, notice how these bass drum hits lock in with the constant sixteenth notes on the hi-hat. You can hear this style of playing in rock and funk drumming.

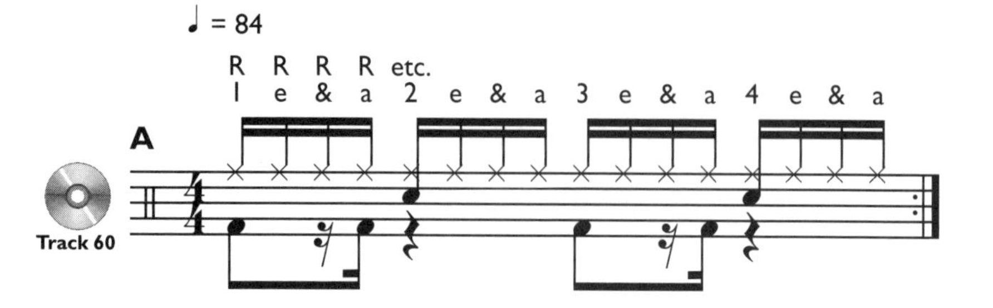

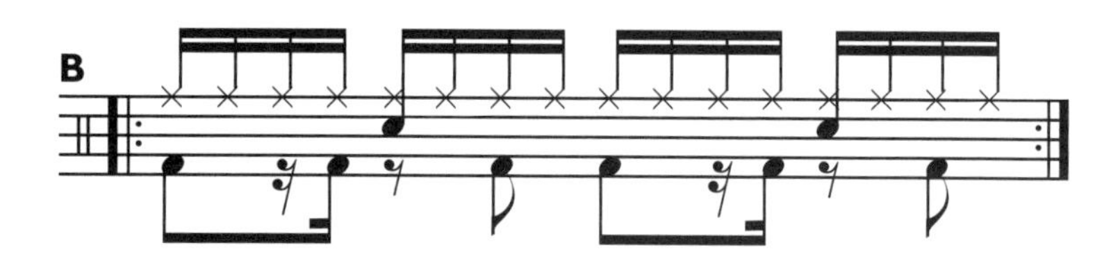

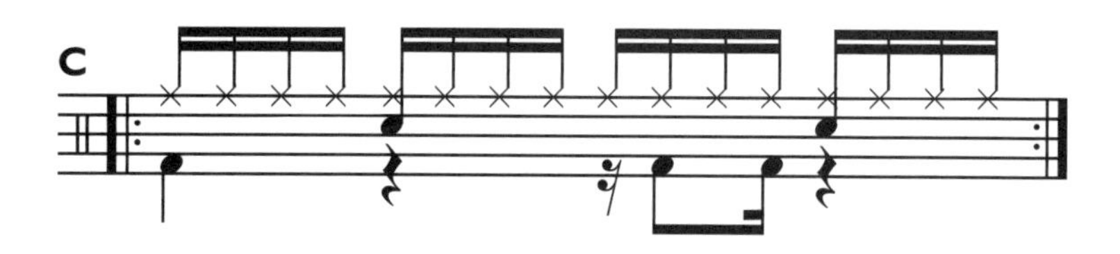

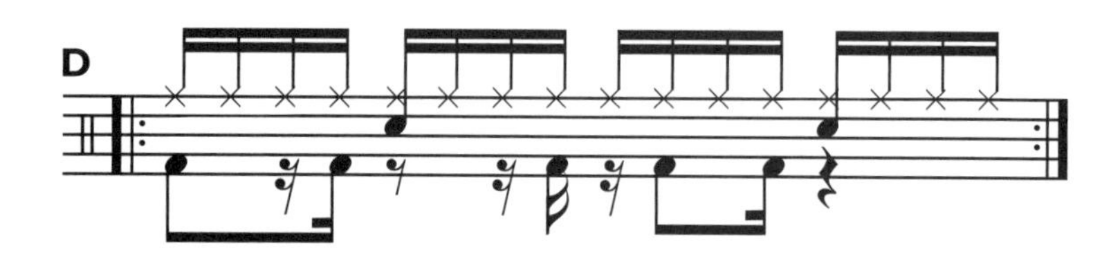

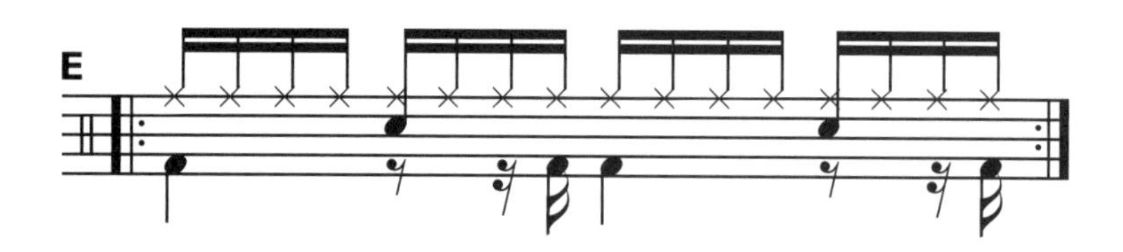

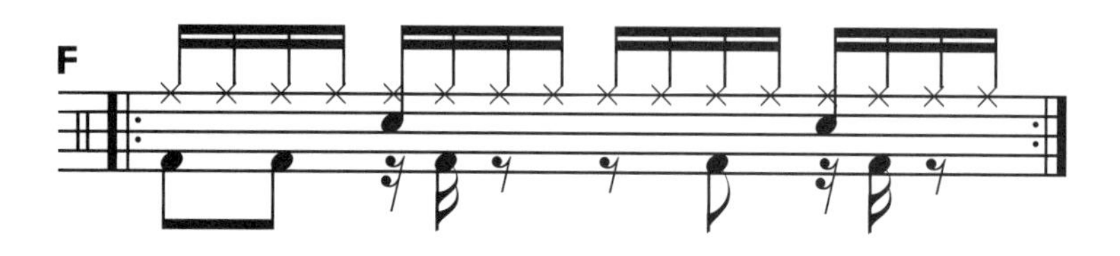

EIGHTH-NOTE HI-HAT WITH MIXED SIXTEENTH-NOTE BEATS

It is time to work on playing eighth notes on the hi-hat with sixteenth notes on either the snare or bass drum. Up to now, we have been playing sixteenth-note beats that have a constant sixteenth note flow on the hi-hat. This has been useful for locking in the offbeats on the snare and bass drum. With eighth notes on the hi-hat, there will no longer be a constant sixteenth note to lock in with, so counting becomes crucial to accurately placing all of the offbeats. Take at look at the next beat. Notice how the snare drum plays on the very last sixteenth of beat 2.

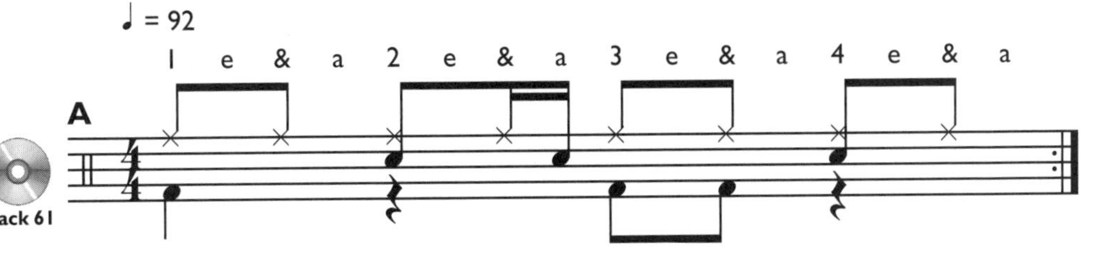

Another way to conceptualize this beat is to put what the hands are doing onto one surface (either a snare drum or drum pad will do).

Here is the same rhythm voiced between the hi-hat and snare with an accent on beats 2 and 4.

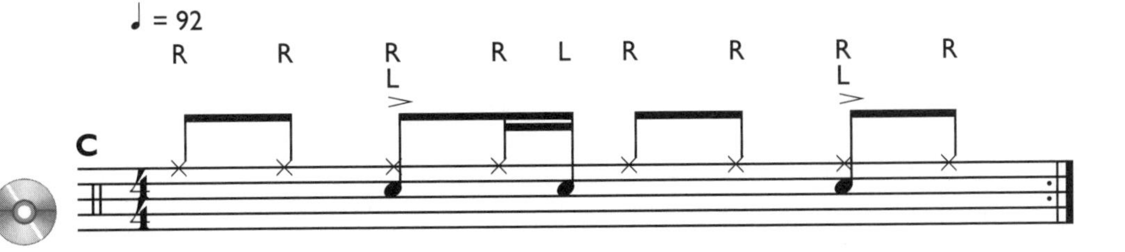

The next section takes this idea further.

CHANGING SIXTEENTH-NOTE RHYTHMS INTO BEATS

You can take written rhythms and make them sound musical by simply orchestrating them around the set. The following examples are sixteenth-note rhythms that, when played between the hi-hat and snare drum, become drumset beats.

RHYTHM TO BEAT CONVERSION EXERCISE NO. 1

Basic Rhythm

♩ = 92

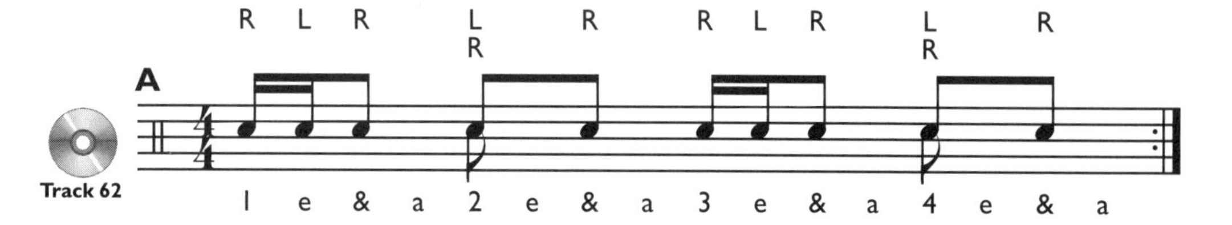

Voiced as a Drumset Beat

♩ = 92

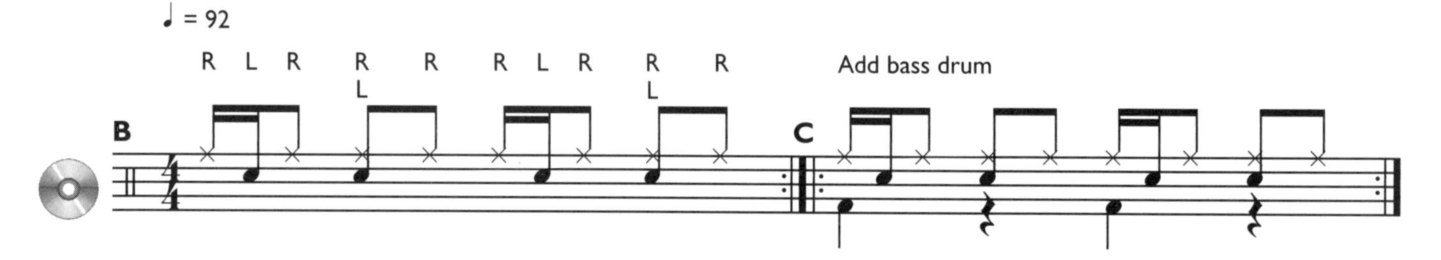

RHYTHM TO BEAT CONVERSION EXERCISE NO. 2

Basic Rhythm

♩ = 92

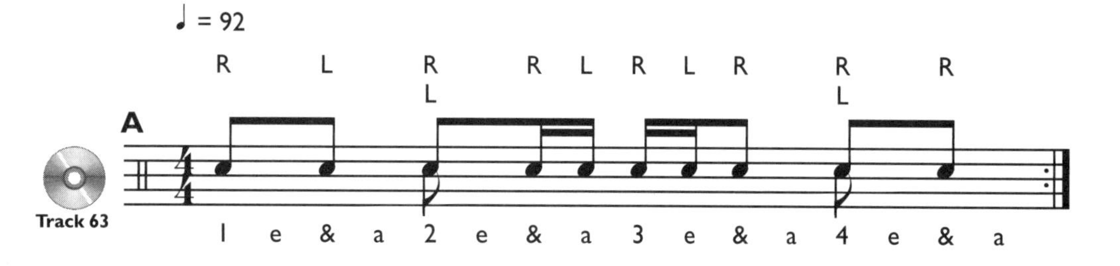

Voiced as a Drumset Beat

♩ = 92

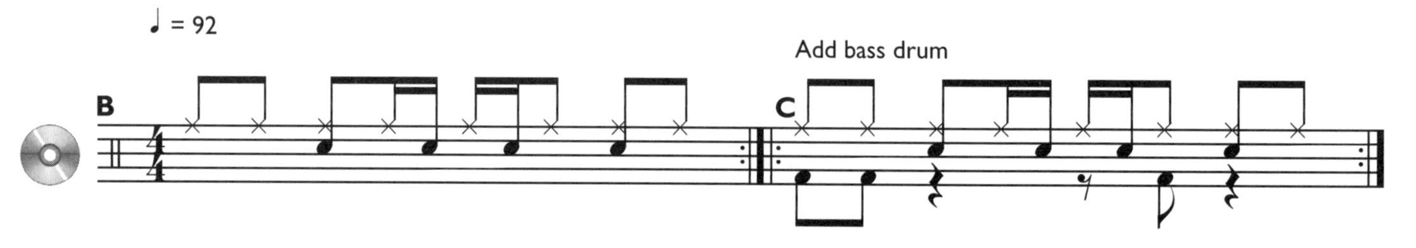

RHYTHM TO BEAT CONVERSION EXERCISE NO. 3

Basic Rhythm

Voiced as a Drumset Beat

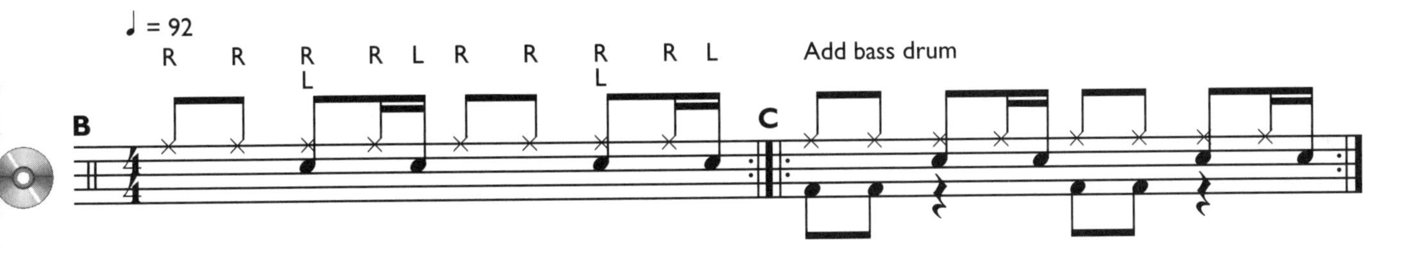

RHYTHM TO BEAT CONVERSION EXERCISE NO. 4

Basic Rhythm

Voiced as a Drumset Beat

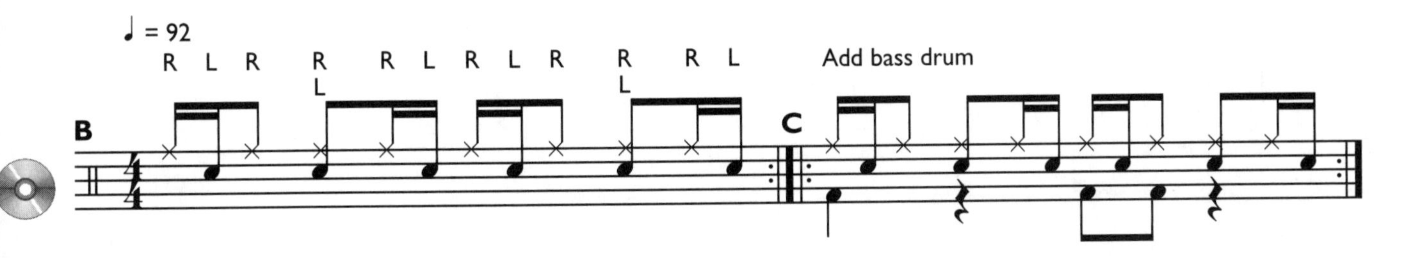

DOTTED NOTES

A dot to the right of a note indicates the note's value is increased by half. A dotted quarter note is worth one beat plus half of that beat (a quarter note plus an eighth note). A dotted quarter note is often followed by an eighth note.

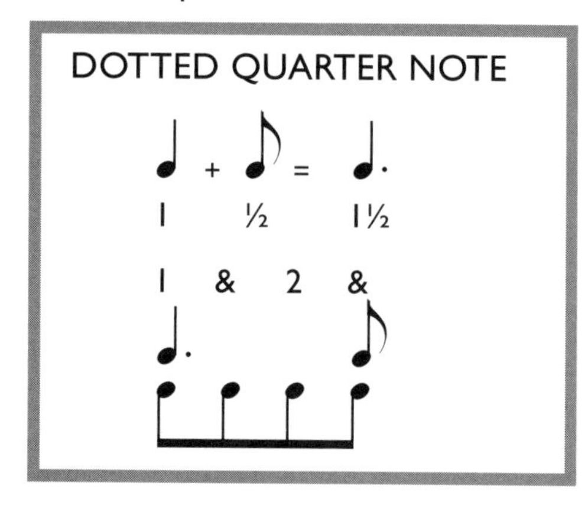

A dotted eighth note is worth an eighth note plus a sixteenth note, or ¾ of a beat (three sixteenth notes). A dotted eighth note is often followed by a sixteenth note.

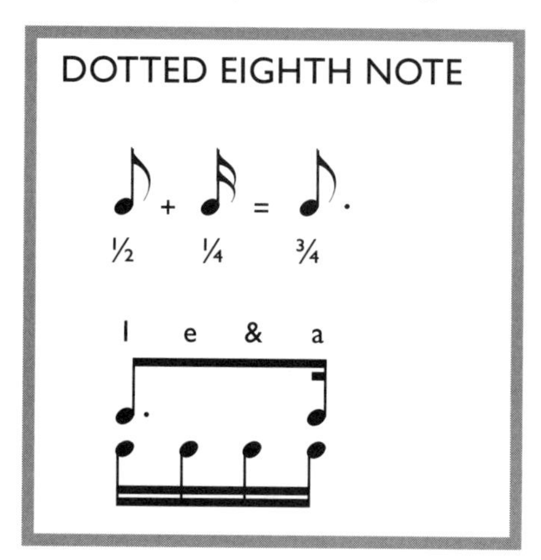

Let's apply this rhythm to the bass drum in some beats.

__Mitch Mitchell__ played the drums with the Jimi Hendrix Experience beginning in 1966 and continued with them until Hendrix's death in 1970. Mitchell's fluid funk/jazz/rock style was a perfect match for Hendrix's superb guitar playing.

PHOTO • JIM CUMMINS/COURTESY OF STAR FILE PHOTO, INC.

TWO SIXTEENTH NOTES ON THE BASS DRUM

The following beats have two consecutive sixteenth notes played with the bass drum. These beats will be challenging, so take your time and master each one accurately before moving on to the next. These beats sound much better when all of the bass drum notes are played at the same volume.

BASS DRUM SIXTEENTH-NOTE EXERCISE NO. 1

Bass Drum Line

Applied to a Beat

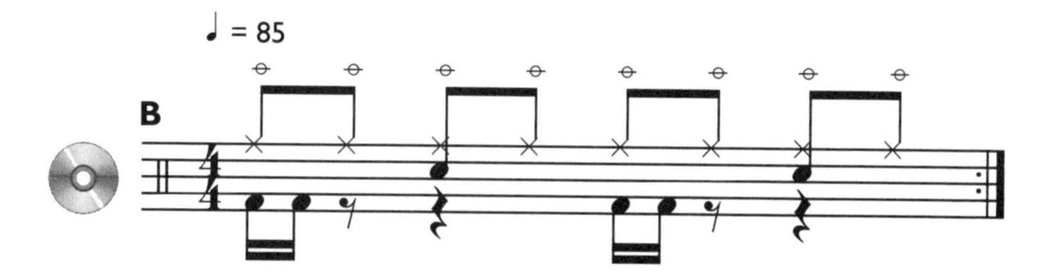

BASS DRUM SIXTEENTH-NOTE EXERCISE NO. 2

Bass Drum Line

Applied to a Beat

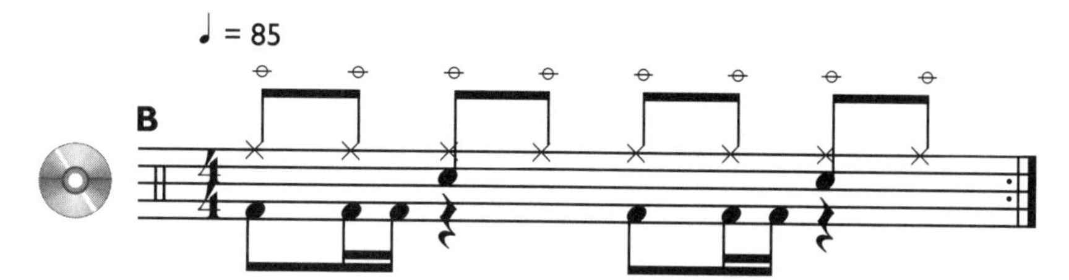

BASS DRUM SIXTEENTH-NOTE EXERCISE NO. 3

Bass Drum Line

♩ = 85

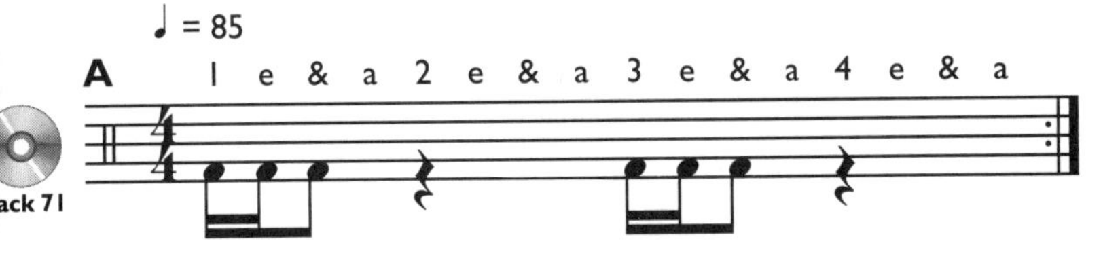

Applied to a Beat

♩ = 85

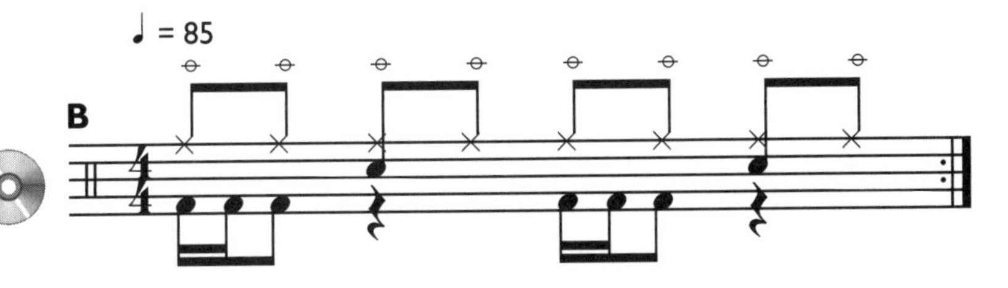

BASS DRUM SIXTEENTH-NOTE EXERCISE NO. 4

Bass Drum Line

♩ = 85

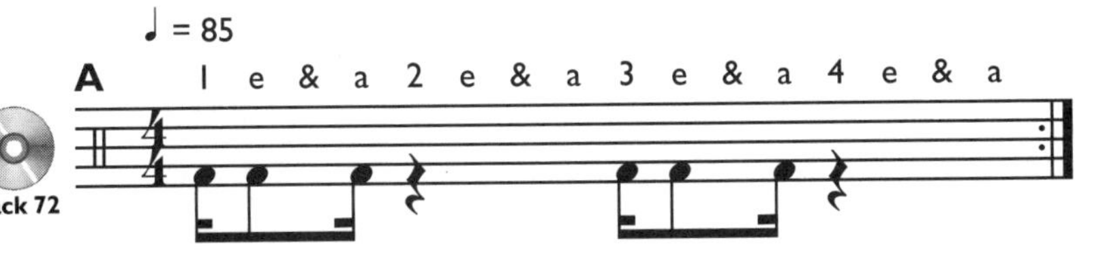

Applied to a Beat

♩ = 85

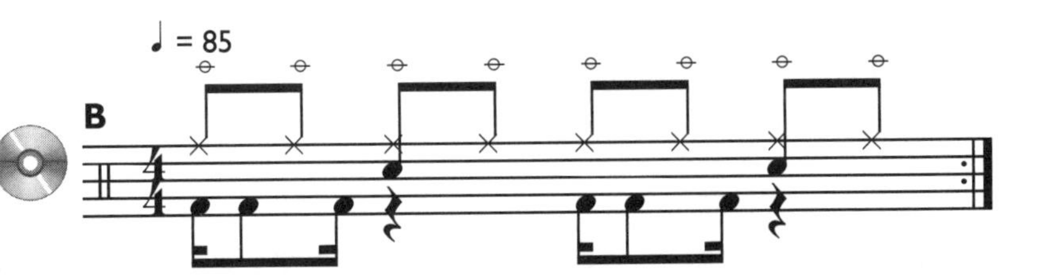

BASS DRUM SIXTEENTH-NOTE EXERCISE NO. 5

Bass Drum Line

♩ = 85

Applied to a Beat

♩ = 85

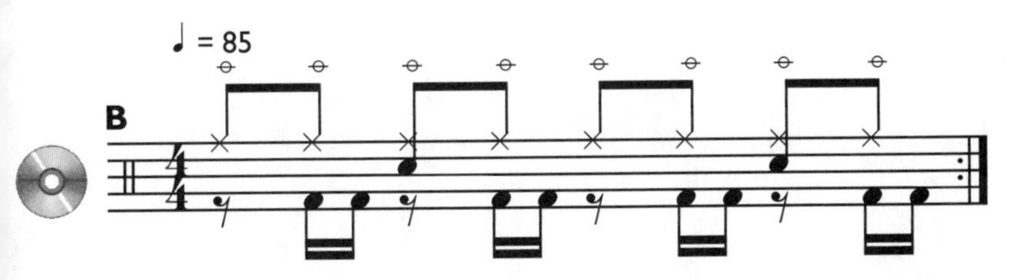

PLAYING OFFBEATS ON THE BASS DRUM

For the purposes of this discussion, the term "offbeat" will refer to the second and fourth sixteenths in every beat—the "e" and the "a" of the sixteenth-note pulse.

This is an exercise that will greatly increase your ability to play offbeat sixteenth notes on the bass drum. To get started, play eighth notes on the hi-hat with the right hand.

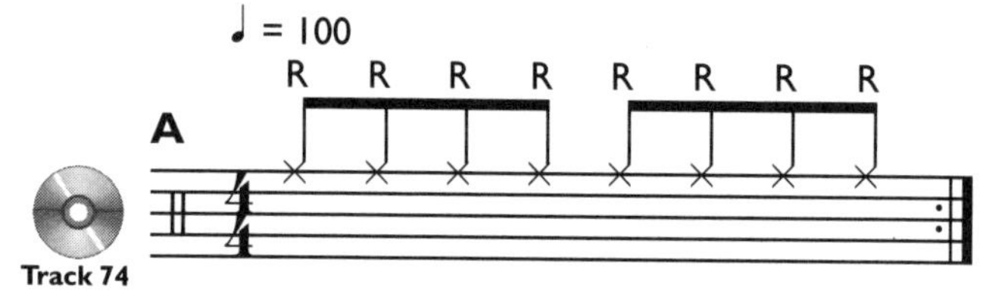

Now play all of the offbeat sixteenth notes on the bass drum. Think of this as a single-stroke roll between your right hand and left foot.

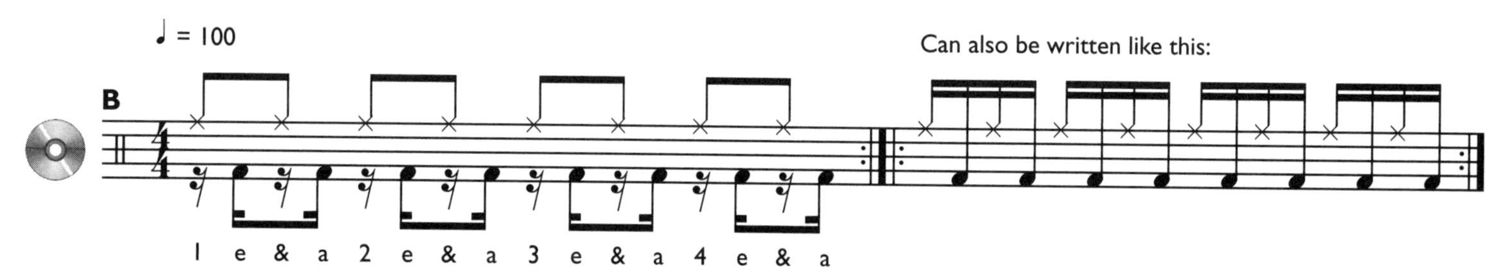

Practice example B with one measure of hi-hat eighth notes before each repetition, as shown in example C.

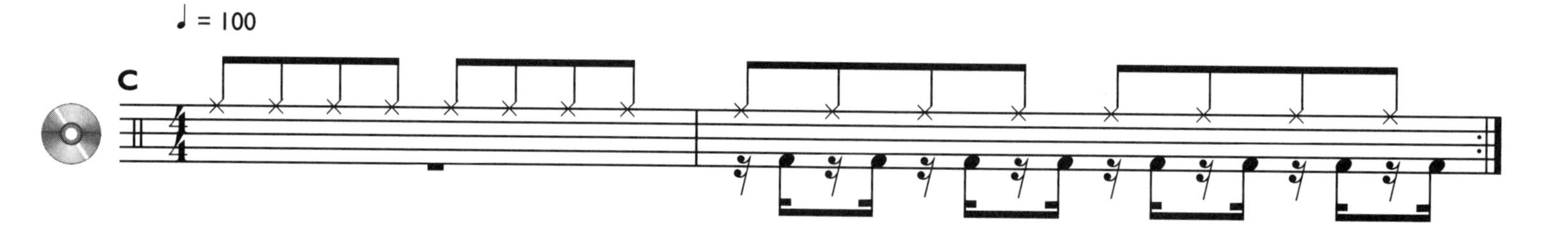

Add the snare drum on beats 2 and 4.

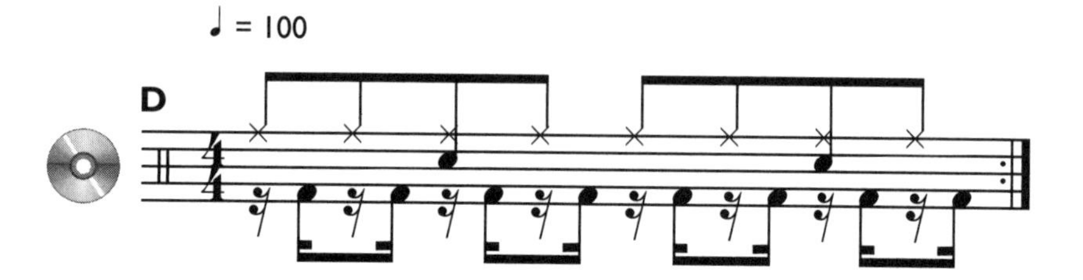

Here are some beats that use the offbeat bass drum. Studying beats like these will enable you to play more complex-sounding grooves in a very confident and accurate manner.

SINGLE SIXTEENTH-NOTE BASS-DRUM EXERCISES

The following series of exercises will sharpen your ability to place a single sixteenth-note bass-drum hit anywhere in a measure while holding down a groove. Again, counting as you play is crucial to the accurate placement of each bass-drum hit.

DOUBLE SIXTEENTH-NOTE BASS-DRUM EXERCISES

The following exercises are an extension of the exercises on page 82. Here, we will concentrate on playing two consecutive bass-drum notes anywhere they can occur in a measure while playing a groove. Some of these variations will sound good in and of themselves, others are useful as practice tools for learning and practicing all of the possibilities.

PROGRESSIVE SIXTEENTH-NOTE BASS-DRUM EXERCISES

Here's an exercise that will greatly increase your bass drum control. The idea is to start off playing one bass-drum note per measure and progressively add another sixteenth note in each measure so by the end of the exercise, you are playing a full measure of sixteenths on the bass drum. Take this slowly at first, otherwise your foot will have great difficulty keeping up!

CHAPTER 9

Getting Started with Drum Fills

In this chapter, we'll take a look at drum *fills* and work on ways to develop a vocabulary of things to play in performance. Drum fills, in their most basic form, are variations of the groove of a song. Listening to enough music will reveal that drum fills are often a way for the drummer to set up the next section of a song.

Song forms come in sections of various lengths. Basic song sections are:

Verse	Tells a story and may change on repetition.
Bridge	Connects two musical passages or themes.
Pre-Chorus	A short section that leads directly into the chorus.
Chorus	The refrain. Usually contains the title of the piece and does not change on repetitions.

By carefully listening to your favorite music, you can easily identify the different sections that make up the songs. As you are listening, pay attention to how the drummer helps mark the change from one section to the next. As a drummer, you must be aware of the form of the songs you are playing and know where and when to add fills. This requires listening skills and a repertoire of drum fills that are relevant to the music you are currently playing.

Your primary obligation is to keep the tempo steady. You don't want to lose the time. Drum fills should add something to the music being played, not take away from it. A fill is not an opportunity to show off your drumming prowess. Many drummers lose the time during fills, either by not coming out of them correctly, or by *rushing* (speeding up) or *dragging* (slowing down). Try to play fills that fit the groove.

To get started, let's work on counting and playing only four measures so we can easily keep track of how many measures have been played and where we are in the form. This is a very important skill that you will need to master.

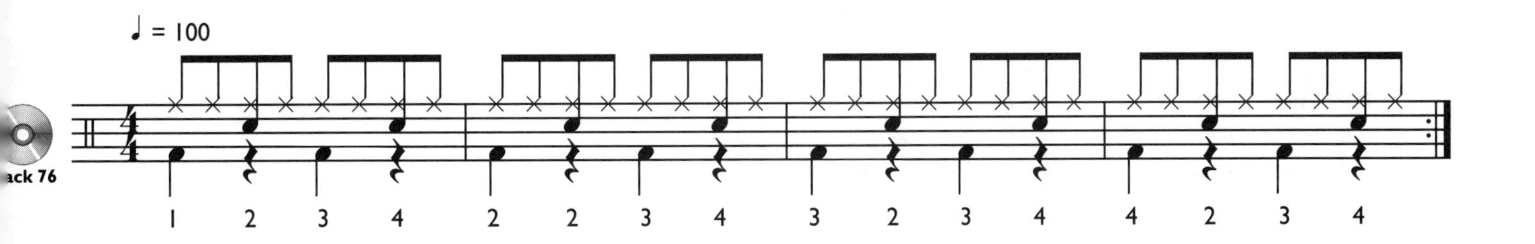

DEVELOPING THE FOUR-BAR PHRASE

The next step will be to play a beat and mark the beginning of each four *bars* (musicians often call a measure a *bar*) with a cymbal crash on beat one of the very first measure. This will give a very obvious, audible cue as to the location of beat 1, called the *downbeat*. Also, notice the style of counting in this example. To help keep track of our place in the form, we number the bars as we go along. This is a commonly-used and useful device.

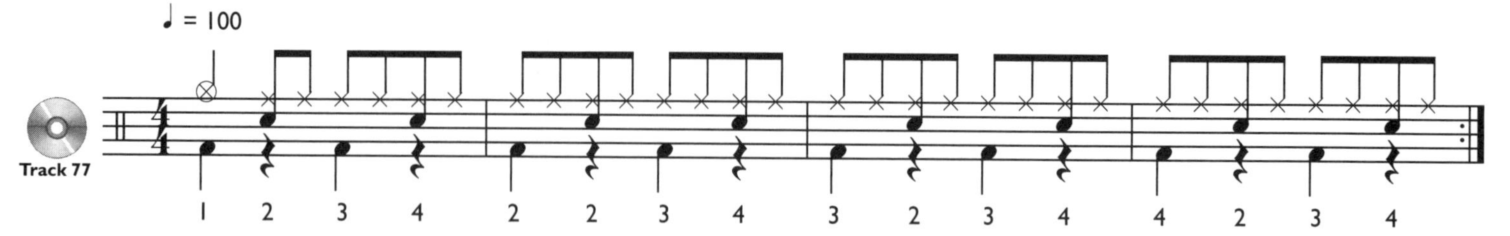

When you can nail the downbeat every time on the crash cymbal, it's time to work on some fills for bar 4 to lead up to the downbeat of bar 1. Think of bar 4 as the "set-up" and the crash on the downbeat of bar 1 as the "resolution."

Here is a three-bar beat. Below it are four choices to use as fills in bar 4. Try adding each of them as bar 4 to the three-bar beat.

THE EIGHTH-NOTE FLOW FOR DRUM FILLS

When you are playing a particular style of drum beat, you should be able to play fills and ideas that come out of the main flow of time you have already established. Let's work on this with an eighth-note hi-hat rock rhythm. Working on examples like these will help you build a vocabulary of fills.

Here is a three-bar eighth-note hi-hat rock rhythm with choices of fills for bar 4. Practice using them all.

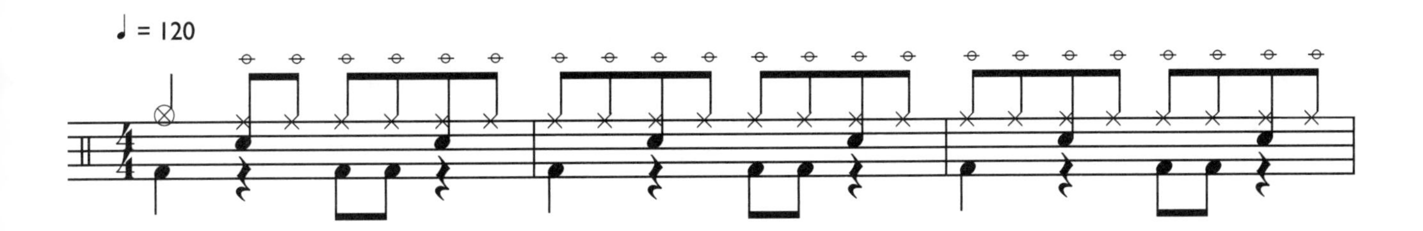

Here are the fills for bar 4:

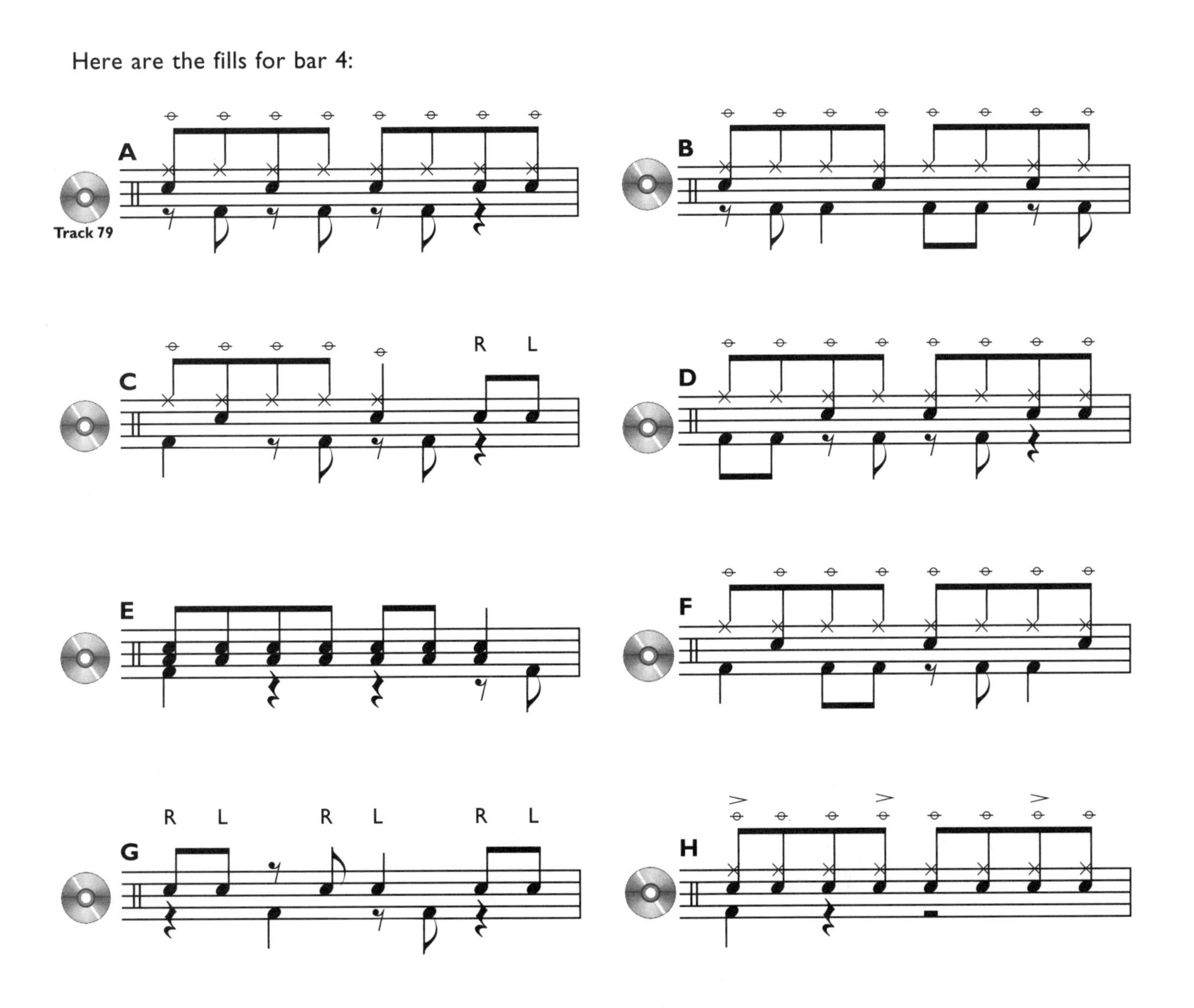

EIGHTH-NOTE FILLS THAT END ON BEAT 4

A common and very effective way to play a fill is to put a hit, often with an accent, on beat 4, just before you crash on the downbeat of bar 1. These fills happen at varying times, from one beat before beat 4, two beats before beat 4, and so on. This will increase your awareness of the possibilities for drum fills.

Here's your beat:

Here are the fills for bar 4:

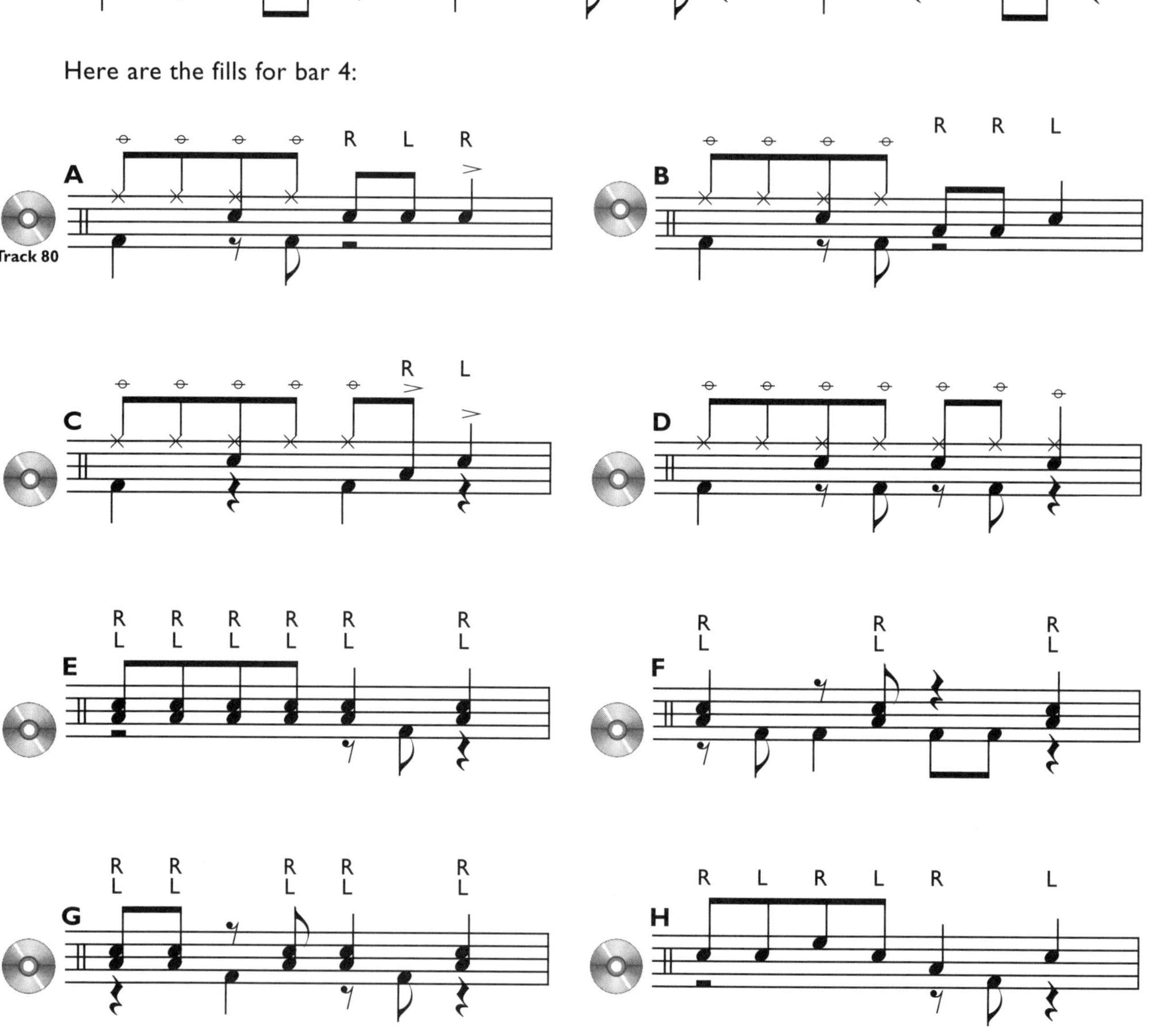

SHORT FILLS USING SIXTEENTH NOTES

The next series of drum fills will use short sixteenth-note ideas. They sound good in many tempos and musical situations, and because they are short and easy to use. Due to the nature of drumset playing, the drummer is often allowed a lot of freedom to improvise. The more musical information you have, the more options you have. Drum fills are often improvised on the spot, so having a repertoire of ideas to draw upon will be very helpful.

Here's your beat for beat 4:

Here are the fills for bar 4:

The following fills will also incorporate the bass drum in some of the ideas. It will be helpful to think of the sixteenth-note flow and to count steady sixteenth notes as you play. The stickings indicated are only suggestions to get you started. Feel free to experiment with some different stickings after you have learned these.

Here's the beat:

Here are the fills for bar 4:

LONGER FILLS USING SIXTEENTH NOTES

The next series of drum fills will take a basic idea and work it through varying lengths of time. We'll start out playing the idea for one beat and progressively expand it to a full measure. There will also be suggestions on how to orchestrate the idea around the set. Examples A, B and C each have one variation. Example D has three variations.

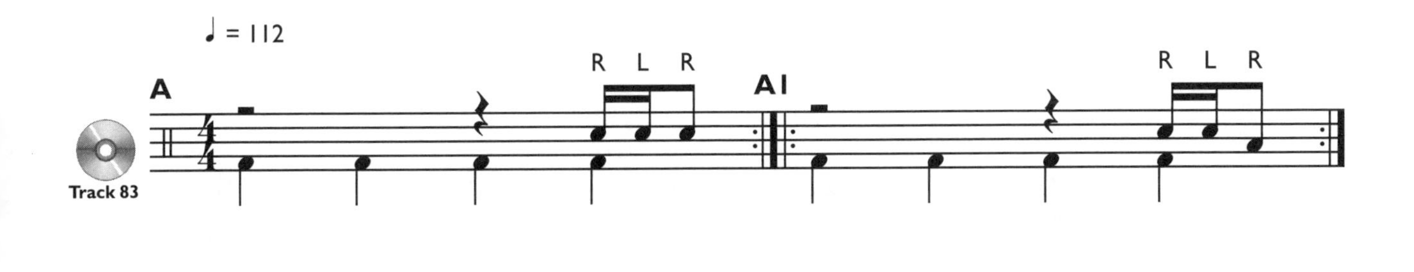

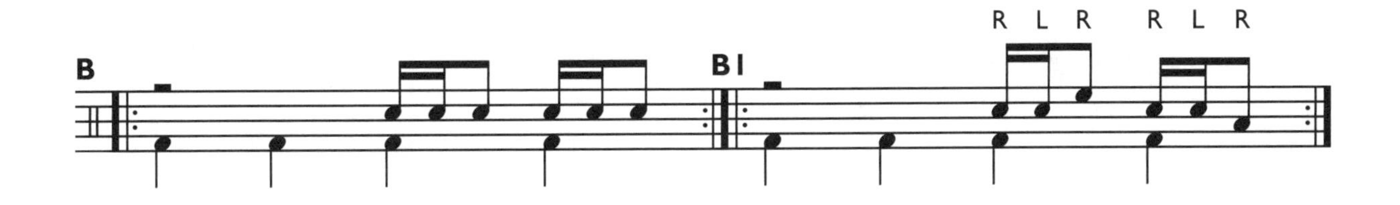

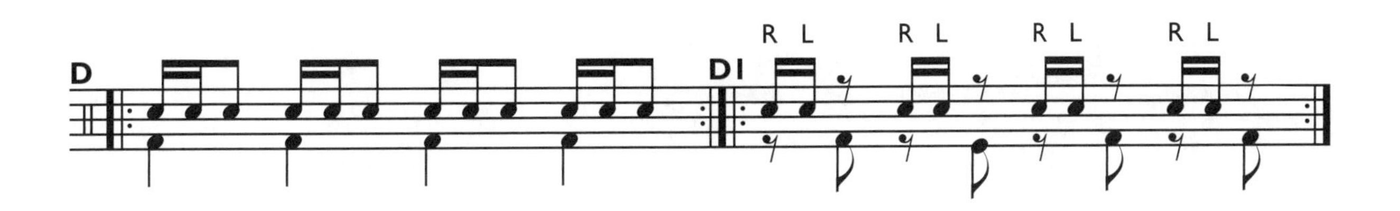

Here is another basic idea that is progressively expanded to fill the measure. Examples A, B and C each have one variation. Example D has four additional variations.

RESOLVING FILLS ON THE "&" OF BEAT 4

Often, fills do not end or resolve on the downbeat. Depending on what's going on in the music and what the other instruments may happen to be accenting, they may end on any part of the measure. In the following examples, we will explore ending drum fills on the "&" of beat 4 in the last measure. This will naturally give the fill an "upbeat" feeling and is quite effective in the right spot. These examples will use a *tied* note, which indicates you are to play the "and" of four on the crash cymbal and allow the note to sustain over the bar to a note in the next measure.

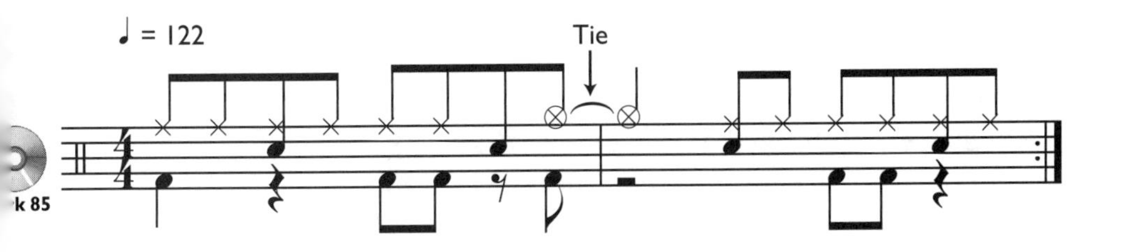

Sometimes a beat or song will begin just before the downbeat of the first full measure. This is called a *pickup*. Here's a beat that begins with a pickup on the "&" of beat 4.

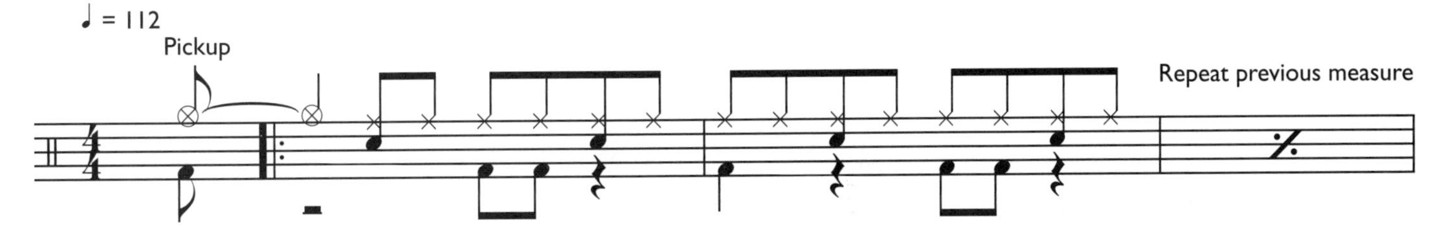

Here are some fills that resolve on the "&" of beat 4. Put them on the end of the beat and then go back to the right-facing repeat.

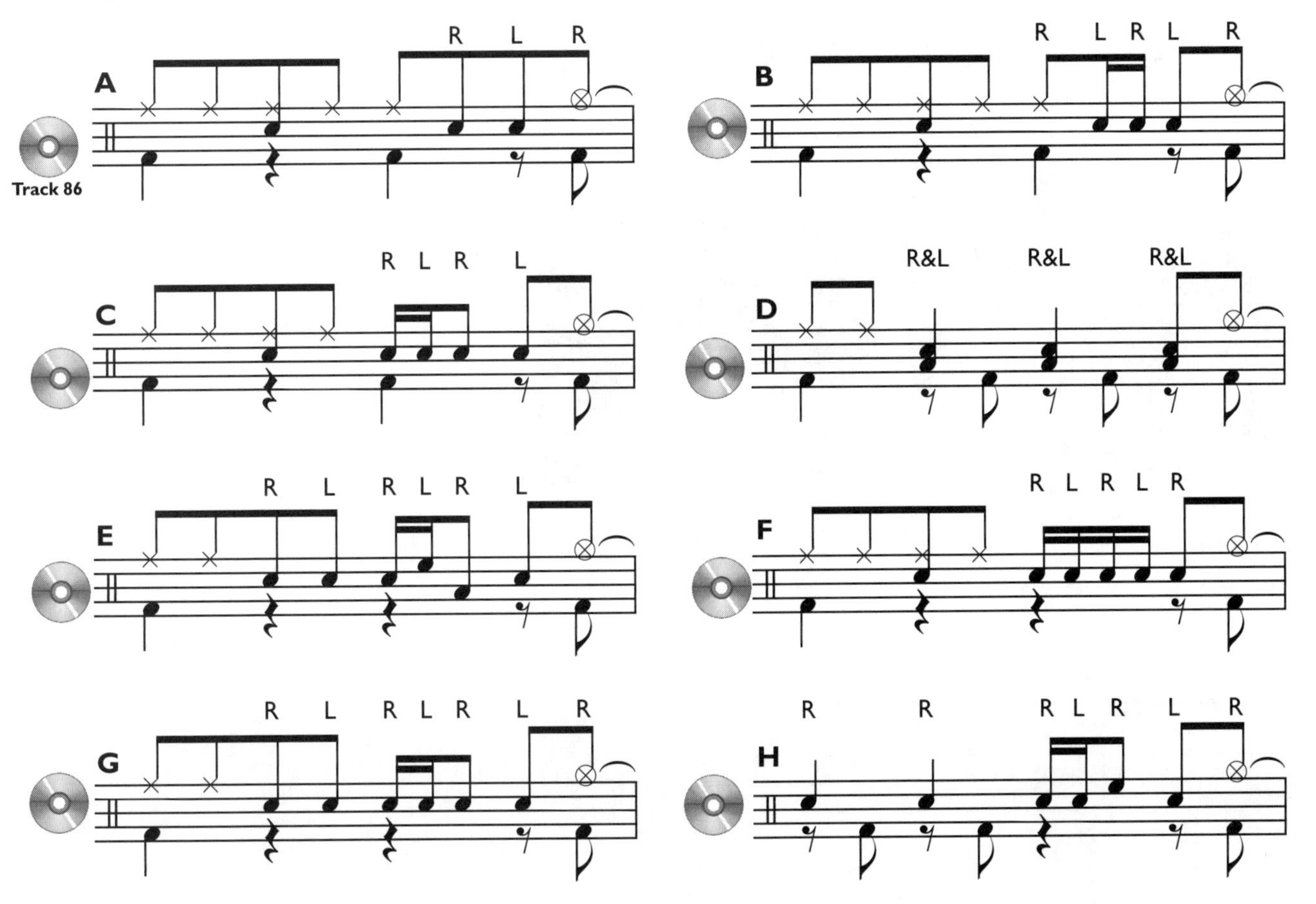

APPENDIX

Joe Morello Interview: Part 1

Joe Morello is one of the greatest jazz drummers of all time. Early on, he played with Phil Woods and Sal Salvador. He played short stints in 1952–1953 with Johnny Smith, Stan Kenton's Orchestra and Gil Melle, but built a good reputation primarily for his work with the Marian McPartland trio (1953–1956). He also played with Tal Farlow and Jimmy Raney during this period.

Morello gained fame as a member of the Dave Brubeck Quartet during 1956–1967, making it possible for Brubeck to experiment with unusual time signatures. It was with Brubeck that he recorded the classic drum feature "Take Five." Joe Morello still plays and participates in occasional reunions with Brubeck and McPartland.

Pete Sweeney studied with Joe Morello for ten years, and sat down with him in 2003 (not long after his 75th birthday) for a discussion. This interview will be spread out over all three volumes in this three-volume method. Enjoy.

Joe Morello and the author, Pete Sweeney

PS: *How did you get started playing drums?*
JM: I actually started off on violin from age five until 12. To this day, some of my favorite music to listen to is classical violin. I would go down to a theater in Springfield, Massachusetts where they had Vaudeville-type shows and I would sit in the front row over the orchestra pit to watch and listen to the drummer, Joe Sefcik. I loved his playing; everything was so loose and nice and I wanted to be able to do that. I began to study with him, and my lessons would be at the theater either in the orchestra pit between shows or in a spare room downstairs where they kept the letters for the marquee. I learned the rudiments and how to read from him, plus a great deal about technical facility. I became his best student because I practiced a lot. I enjoyed it.

PS: *What was your first drumset like?*
JM: I didn't have a full set at first. I sold Christmas cards one year and saved up enough money to buy a Ludwig snare with a wire stand. I played my first gig with just that snare drum, no bass drum or anything. It was at a place called the Widow's Club with a piano player for a dollar. After that my cousin loaned me a set when he went into the Army. It had a huge bass drum and tiny cymbals. Eventually I made enough money to buy my own set.

PS: *You have studied with some of the greatest teachers of all time, people like George Lawrence Stone and Billy Gladstone. How important is it for someone starting out to get a private teacher?*
JM: Getting a good, qualified teacher will save you time by pointing you in the right direction when you're learning. It's also a great idea to play with a school band. It gives you experience playing with other people and teaches you how to work together as a team. Another important thing would be to study some basic piano and learn the rudiments of music like reading the clefs and basic chord structures.

PS: *What are your thoughts about practicing with a metronome?*
JM: The metronome is great for helping you with accuracy. It gives you even spacing, and can be used to develop your facility. It's good to practice different tempos with, and can show you where your weaknesses are. A good exercise is to play with a metronome for a while, then turn it off and continue to play. Eventually turn the metronome back on and see if you stayed at the tempo you started with.